MEGA-TEACHING AND LEARNING

NEUROLINGUISTIC PROGRAMMING APPLIED TO EDUCATION

**C. Van Nagel
Edward J. Reese
Maryann Reese
Robert Siudzinski**

Metamorphous Press
Portland, OR

Published by

Metamorphous Press
P.O. Box 10616
Portland, OR 97210-0616

Copyright © 1985 by C. Van Nagel, Edward J. Reese,
Maryann Reese, and Robert Siudzinski
Editorial and Art Direction by Lori Stephens
Printed in the United States of America

Mega-teaching and learning : neurolinguistic programming applied
to education / C. Van Nagel . . . [et al.].
p.   cm.
Originally published: Indian Rock Beach, FL : Southern Institute Press, 1985.
Includes bibliographical references (p.) and index.
ISBN 1-55552-018-9 : $14.95
1. Learning. 2. Cognition in children. 3. Paired-association learning. 4. Neurolinguistic
programming. I. Van Nagel, C.
LB1060.M44   1993
370.15'23--dc20   93-26741

ACKNOWLEDGEMENTS

We wish to acknowledge the assistance of Jackie Tatum for the editing and typing of
this book.

CONTENTS

FOREWORD

The application of Neuro Linguistic Programming techniques and strategies to education provides a fresh and innovative approach to teaching and learning. As such, it will revolutionize the way you think about teaching and learning. The possibilities of learning and behavior change contained within this book will open new horizons to you and your students.

This piece of work is by far one of the most outstanding contributions to the field of education in the last decade.

Richard Bandler
Co-Developer of
Neuro Linguistic Programming

ABOUT THE AUTHORS

C. VAN NAGEL, PH.D.

Dr. C. Van Nagel received his Ph.D. from the University of Pittsburgh. He is a licensed psychologist, Pennsylvania licensure, who has lectured both nationally and internationally. His work with the competency-based teacher training programs has won the American Association College Teacher Education Award and the Florida Teacher Education Award. In 1981, his research on vocational training for the disadvantaged was selected by the Michigan Project (funded by the U.S. Departments of Labor and Justice) to be filmed and disseminated throughout the United States. Dr. Van Nagel has state, national and international publications that deal with training individuals for increased performance and achievement. Dr. Van Nagel has been selected by twelve major educational associations to be their keynote speaker. He has thirty-three publications on learning and behavior development and is one of the most sought-after trainers and speakers in the United States. In 1989, he received The National University Continuing Education Award for his outstanding presentations and program development and in 1990, he was selected by students and colleagues at the University of North Florida to receive the outstanding teacher education award.

ROBERT SIUDZINSKI, PH.D.

Dr. Siudzinski is Director of Special Education, University of North Florida, Jacksonville, Florida. Having received his Ph.D. degree from Arizona State University in 1966. He has worked extensively in the area of behavioral management and special education. He assumed the charter chairmanship of the Special Education Program at the University of North Florida in 1972. Under Dr. Siudzinski's direction, the program achieved national reputation in 1979 when it was one of only three programs in the United States awarded the American Association of Colleges of Teacher Education Award for Excellence in Teacher Education. At the state level, the Florida Association of Teacher Education recognized the undergraduate program by selecting it as the Outstanding University Teacher Preparation Program for 1980-81. He is a certified Master Practitioner of NLP.

EDWARD J. REESE, M.S.W., ACSW

Mr. Reese is President and co-founder of the Southern Institute of NLP and Vice-President of International NLP. He is a certified Trainer of NLP, an adjunct faculty member at the University of Miami, School of Medicine. He is a full member of AGPA, a member of the Academy of Certified Social Workers, and a member of International Association of Neuro-Linguistic Programming, and a member of National Associate of Social Workers, diplomate in Clinical Social Work.

Mr. Reese is a licensed clinical social worker by the Florida Department of Professional Regulation. He received his Master's of Social Work from Rutgers University School of Social Work.

MARYANN REESE, M.S.W.

Ms. Reese is Executive Director and co-founder of the Southern Institute of NLP and President of International NLP. She is a certified Trainer of NLP and an adjunct professor at the University of North Florida. She is a licensed Family and Marriage Counselor of the State of Florida, and a consultant and trainer for Success Sciences of Tampa, Florida. She is a member of American Marriage and Family Association and the International Association of Neuro-Linguistic Programming.

Ms. Reese has presented both nationally and internationally. She received her Master's degree from Seton Hall University, New Jersey.

AUTHORS' NOTE

Dear Educator:

You are the one who has the power to use the information and skills in this book to inspire, motivate, and teach students. You are the one who can help students to try, to practice, and to perfect the skills they need to become the special people they are capable of becoming!

As you read and study each chapter, put yourself totally into the task of understanding and applying the skills. You will then see at once how to use what you read and how you can bring life to the words in your own classroom. Your knowledge of how to use the techniques will increase, building upon your present skills. Your skills in giving students reinforcement for their efforts, in helping them to develop the courage to try another way, and in helping them to maintain the determination to perfect and master what is needed will greatly expand with these techniques.

This book contains the most effective and powerful teaching/learning tools presently known! How they are used in the future is up to you. You may use these tools as specifically described in this book. You may also choose to create new applications or techniques, which may lift us to even higher levels of understanding and learning! We hope that you will share these with us.

Remember this: the future of education is in your hands. What do you see? What are the possibilities for you and for others as you use the tools and techniques in this book?

Our sincere best wishes to you as you grow and succeed in your contributions to students and others.

C. Van Nagel
Edward J. Reese
Maryann Reese
Robert Siudzinski

WHAT IS NEURO LINGUISTIC PROGRAMMING?

Neuro Linguistic Programming is a model of human behavior and communication. It involves how people represent, decode, and process incoming and outgoing behavior. As such, it includes studies of perception and behavior which make our behavior possible. In Neuro Linguistic Programming (NLP), the total organism and its environment are studied.

In essence, NLP studies the neurolinguistic process and its interaction with the environment. As these processes interact, they are represented, organized, and sequenced into patterns and models of language and behavior which are stored in an individual. These stored neural patterns become a basis for influencing future behavior.

INTRODUCTION:
HOW TO USE THIS BOOK

The focus of this book is on teachers and students. However, the principles and techniques are applicable to any person or population.

We have adopted a format in this book to enhance comprehension and retention of the content. Advanced organizers in the form of concepts and vocabularies with brief explanations are placed at the beginning of each chapter to permit the reader to enter a part of our model of the world. Research has shown that such an approach greatly enhances comprehension of the material about to be read.

Each chapter is written in a developmental way, so as to enable the reader to progress through the various levels of concepts with ease. Many of the chapters have exercises within the chapter text or at the end of the chapter. This should enable the reader to apply skills in an experiential way.

It is important that the reader begin with the first chapter of the book and read through to the end without skipping any chapters. After reading a chapter, the reader should do the exercises at the end of the chapter. Doing the exercises according to the arranged levels will promote a thorough understanding of the chapter, as well as provide a foundation for the next chapter.

As we recognize that a book such as this is not a substitute for professional training, we advise you to obtain further training. By attending special training sessions and workshops, you will enhance your skills.

As our research progresses, we will share our new discoveries with you. We invite you to share with us your successes and observations. The authors welcome any individual to contribute to our growing field of knowledge and research. Those who do so will be acknowledged in future publications.

MEGA-TEACHING AND LEARNING

Chapter 1
The Importance
Of Rapport

ADVANCED ORGANIZER

OVERVIEW

In this chapter, you will learn the relationship and importance of rapport as it impacts on motivation and the learning process. The steps required to establish rapport will be described. Exercises will be provided to enable you to observe your progress and insure your success.

CONCEPTS

Rapport—A relationship between individuals that is characterized by harmony, understanding, and mutual confidence. This type of relationship is desirable between the student and the teacher for maximum learning.

Pacing—Pacing involves feeding back the vocabulary of the most highly valued representational system to the individual as well as feeding back or matching body movements, eye blinks, etc.

Mirroring—The teacher reflects the student's eye blinks, posture, breathing patterns, body movements, language, etc. Example: When the student's eyes blink, the teacher also blinks the eyes; or, when the student moves an arm or leg, the teacher makes the same movement.

Leading—A process of changing a student's behavior patterns by matching and pacing the behavior and then changing some aspect of your behavior which, in turn, influences the student's behavior. Example: The teacher matches the student's rapid breathing rate, then slows the rate gradually until a more normal breathing rate is realized.

Representational System—Representational systems refer to auditory, visual, kinesthetic, olfactory, and gustatory senses that students use to create their particular models of the world. For example: 1) An auditory student processes primarily by listening and emphasizes the spoken words for communication; 2) A visual student prefers to use the eyes to perceive the world and uses visual images in remembering and thinking; 3) A kinesthetic student prefers to feel experiences by external and internal stimuli which are sorted through feelings; a kinesthetic person's decisions are based primarily on feelings.

VOCABULARY

Calibration—Reading an individual's external state in an inter-action with the individual's observable behavioral cues in his/her external state.

Categorizing—The process of placing an event or behavior in a group or division.

Competence—Achieving a predetermined criterion level.

Confidence—An internal state which allows an individual to perceive that all internal checks are compatible with environmental demands.

Cross-Over Mirroring—The process by which one person matches the specific behavior of another person, but in a different mode. Example: The breathing rate may be matched with a compatible rhythmic foot or leg swing.

Feedback—Information transmitted as a function of individual perceptions of a given stimulus and/or situation.

Feedback Loop—The result of a stimulus-response chain in which a stimulus elicits a response which serves as a confirmation of the relationship.

Predicates—Verbs, adverbs, and adjectives that can be categorized into one or more of the representational systems.

Speech Patterns—Recurring aspects of speech and/or verbal behavior that can be grouped or categorized into personalized patterns.

Sorts/Sorting—The method used to organize or categorize an individual's observations and reactions. Example: When assessing a situation, an individual may sort for positives and not negatives.

Tonality—The quality of an individual's voice, reflected by pitch, volume, nasality, etc.

THE IMPORTANCE OF RAPPORT

Rapport is the foundation of good teaching. Although rapport is frequently identified as an important variable in the literature, there is very little research about how to establish and maintain rapport! This chapter illustrates a step by step procedure for establishing and maintaining rapport.

Rapport, relating, and communication are terms that are characteristic of getting along with people. In this chapter, the teacher will be provided with new concepts of human behavior and with new skills and techniques for shaping behavior. Thus, the teacher will be able to motivate and teach students more effectively and efficiently. Students will, in turn, achieve dramatic results by improving their academic performance and behavior.

The following steps will help to develop skills in establishing rapport and effective communication. In fact, they are applicable to all relationships!

LEVEL I: THE IMPORTANCE OF
RAPPORT TO MOTIVATION

Have you ever done well in some area of learning, not because you liked the subject, but because you liked the teacher or instructor? Have you ever defended an other person's point of view, not because you agreed with him or her, but because you liked or cared for that person? Have you ever wondered why you liked certain individuals? Think about it. Most likely, you will find that the main ingredient was some similarity that you shared or wanted to share with that person (see Illustration 1).

Webster (1985) defines "rapport" as a relationship marked by harmony, conformity, accord, or affinity. When one wants to have good rapport, one has to be in accord or harmony with the other person. In essence, one has to have something in common, or one has to create a common basis. When a commonality is created, the beginning of a relationship is also created. This relationship creates a condition which is conducive to learning.

When a teacher and a student are in harmony or accord, it is much easier to teach the student. Both the teacher and the student may then move more easily toward mutual goals. Energies can be synchronized to reach higher levels of achievement and desirable behaviors. Rapport is a framework for motivation. By achieving rapport, a foundation is provided for effective teaching.

This philosophy is in accord with many historical and philosophical beliefs. For example, aikido, an oriental philosophy and form of self-defense, has demonstrated that even the smallest person can control a large, aggressive person. The smaller person must learn how to blend with, redirect, and be in harmony with the larger person's energy. Similarly, if the teacher develops harmony with the student, the student's behavior can be redirected into productive actions and learning. The student can be led into new experiences and knowledge.

In education, teaching is leading another person to new learnings. The word "education" comes from the Latin word *educare*. *Educare* means "to lead out of ignorance." It is the teacher's purpose to lead students into new levels of awareness and learning, and to help them become successful, constructive, creative, and calm persons. Success yields productive persons who have learned to satisfy their needs in an acceptable way, while facilitating the growth of society as a whole. Successful individuals are able to work both individually and in groups and to be in harmony with others.

Where does one begin? How can one create rapport? In order to be in accord or harmony with students, the teacher must create a similarity or commonality with them. It is not necessary to act,

DO YOU EVER WONDER WHY YOU LIKE CERTAIN
INDIVIDUALS? USUALLY IT IS BECAUSE OF
SOME SIMILARITY YOU SHARE WITH THAT PERSON.

Illustration 1

speak, or dress to imitate student fads in behavior, language, or dress. This similarity or commonality can be accomplished via "mirroring," which is a fundamental aspect of rapport. Mirroring means that some aspects of the student's behavior are matched or imitated by the teacher, thus reflecting the behavior back to the student like a mirror. For example, if a student touches the forehead, the teacher also touches the forehead; if the student breathes slowly, the teacher breathes slowly. It is important that this mirroring be done as casually and unobtrusively as possible.

This mirroring of behavior, when carried out over a period of time, is called "pacing."

Pacing is a significant means for establishing rapport and it can set the foundation for a relationship. In fact, rapport is created by pacing. Most people feel comfortable around people whose behavior and characteristics are similar to their own behavior.

There are several ways in which a person can be mirrored and paced: breathing, body movement, speech patterns, gestures, facial expressions, tempo, tonality, volume of speech, etc. At this time, mirroring and pacing will be discussed as they apply to breathing and body movement. Mirroring and pacing these important areas can provide a solid foundation for establishing and maintaining rapport. Rapport is the first step for creating a climate for learning. Through the rapport that is created, the student can be led into new heights of awareness and learning.

When meeting a student for the first time, notice the student's breathing and body movements. Listen to the student and categorize the student's areas of interests. In observing the breathing, watch the student's shoulders as they rise and fall, or watch the wrinkles move in the student's shirt as the student breathes, then match the breathing pattern. The rise and fall of jewelry, scarfs, collars, or anything worn around the neck may also be observed and matched. The location of breathing (e.g., upper chest level, diaphragm level, or abdominal level) may also be noted. It is important to pace or match both the rhythm of the student's breathing and the location of the breathing.

After observing and matching the breathing for a while, the body movements may be observed unobtrusively in order to match them. For example: If a student crosses both arms, the teacher should unobtrusively cross both arms; if the student shakes a foot, the teacher should also shake a foot. **These observations and actions must be done slowly and casually;** otherwise, they will be interpreted as mockery. These subtle actions will be picked up at the student's subconscious level. When the student's actions are reflected in this way, the teacher is in accord or in harmony with the student at a subconscious level.

These procedures will have a profound effect on building rapport. Mirroring the student's breathing and body movements creates a condition that enables the teacher to influence or change the student's behavior. It is important to remember that pacing by mirroring a student's behavior **over a period of time** results in a state of being in accord or in harmony with that student.

Having begun mirroring and pacing the student, it is time to expand and determine the student's interests. Talking about areas of interests may further develop a commonality between the teacher and the student. This type of pacing is available to the student's awareness or conscious mind. The teacher begins this procedure by closely listening to what the student is talking about. Sort (in your mind) what the student says into categories of interests and notice what area of interest is repeated.

Initially, the Sorting Interest Guides Inventory (see Appendix 1) may be helpful. Later, you will be able to categorize interests automatically. Categorizing will reveal dominant themes that motivate a particular individual, which can be used to establish rapport.

The teacher sometimes may need to ask the student questions to determine specific areas of interests and themes. Some questions which may be asked are: What hobbies do you have? If you could buy three things, what would you buy? What do you like to do? What makes you happy? The teacher also may use personal clues (such as a badge, patch, ring, style of clothes worn, etc.) to elicit conversation and to further define areas of interest.

The answers to these inquiries usually will give an enormous amount of information as to the student's areas of interests. By sorting and categorizing these interests, the teacher is able to communicate with the student on a personal level.

Another form of mirroring and pacing is to reflect the same words and verbal expressions that the student uses. This is done by simply reflecting back, either specifically or similarly, the student's words or the content of what has been said. Simple reflection, either specific or similar, of the student's words or general content of what was said establishes rapport. The student is given the message, "I hear what you are saying; I am connected to your world; I care." Watch for particular words that the student uses to describe events. For example, if the student frequently uses the word "super," weave the word "super" into your verbal expressions and speech patterns.

Mirroring and pacing may include a combination of movement and speech patterns with a matching and blending of both behaviors by the teacher. Picture a student nodding the head up and down and saying, "I can really understand." The teacher may pace by nodding the head up and down and reflecting a similar statement back to the student (e.g., "Yes, I understand that."). Pacing may be compared to the feeling of stepping inside the student's body and being that student. In essence, the teacher is in harmony with the student, so that the student may be led into new areas of growth and development.

Having learned and practiced how to pace breathing, body movements, areas of interests, and speech patterns, the pacing may be expanded to include the following: eye blinks, tonality, and volume of speech. Refer to the exercises at the end of this chapter to further develop skills in mirroring and pacing.

Practice the exercises until a feeling of confidence and competence is experienced consistently at this level, then proceed to the next level.

LEVEL II: MORE ABOUT PACING

Pacing not only builds rapport; pacing also establishes a bond between the teacher and the student. In essence, the teacher enters into the student's model and reflection of the world. Each unique belief system constitutes the whats, hows, and whys of that particular person. When the teacher makes the attempt to join the student's model of the world, the teacher says, "I like you, I am trying to understand you, and I can be in harmony with you without threat." Pacing is a method of establishing rapport, commonality, comfort zones, communication, and possibly even trust and credibility.

Undesirable or unusual behaviors also may be paced. Behaviors such as irregular breathing, asthmatic breathing, tics, and inappropriate language **must** be paced differently. Cross-over mirroring is used in these instances. Cross-over mirroring occurs when the student's behavior is mirrored using a different response. For example, instead of the teacher mirroring the student's irregular breathing, the teacher mirrors the breathing with the movement of a finger. It is most important to keep the same rhythm. When the student's breathing slows down, the teacher's finger movement also must slow down. This pacing is critical to establishing rapport.

Cross-over mirroring for a period of time is called cross-pacing. This is the same pattern as mirroring and pacing, except that the teacher uses cross-over mirroring in the pacing.

A variety of other movements may be used for pacing breathing, such as movement of the head, swinging the leg, or whatever seems natural in the particular situation. The cross-over technique allows the student's behavior to be paced without actually imitating the student's maladaptive behavior. (It has been found that some persons may actually acquire the maladaptive behavior themselves as a result of the process of pacing. However, this is not commonly experienced.)

Cross-over mirroring also may be used to prevent pacing from being perceived as mockery of the student. For example, if a student is breathing rapidly, the teacher might match the rhythm of the student's breathing with the movement of a finger or foot. This is another example of cross-over mirroring.

Practice the exercises marked Level II until confidence and competence are experienced and demonstrated consistently. These exercises will develop rapport-building skills and validate the power in mirroring and pacing. As with any other empirical science, proof of the constructive results of these techniques can best be verified by the experience itself. (See Illustration 2.)

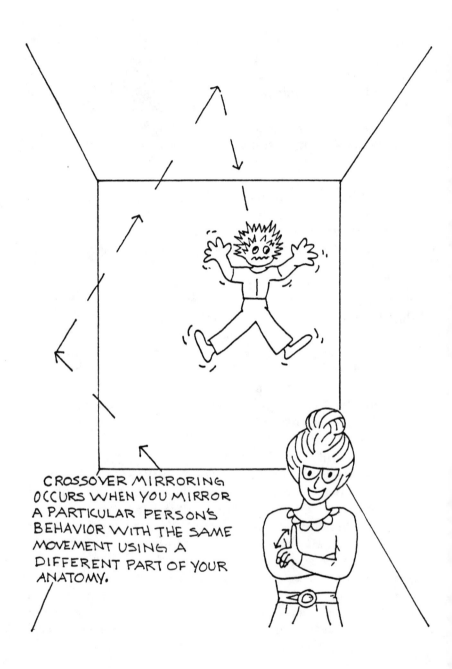

CROSSOVER MIRRORING
OCCURS WHEN YOU MIRROR
A PARTICULAR PERSON'S
BEHAVIOR WITH THE SAME
MOVEMENT USING A
DIFFERENT PART OF YOUR
ANATOMY.

Illustration 2

LEVEL III: LEADING AND BEHAVIOR CHANGE

After learning to mirror and pace a student's behavior, the next step is to lead the student into new or different behaviors. Leading can be compared to changing a step in dancing. For example, the other person's movements in dancing may be paced; the partner pacing (following) may decide to take the lead and introduce a new step. This can be done smoothly and successfully if good pacing is accomplished. Remember: At the beginning, the teacher mirrors until it becomes pace; then the teacher paces, paces, paces, and finally leads. The pattern is to be **repeated** over and over again: Mirror, pace, pace, pace, lead; then mirror, pace, pace, pace, and lead again.

Much pacing must occur before leading. For example, after pacing a student's breathing, body movement, and volume of speech for some time, try moving one hand a certain way and observe whether the student moves a hand in a similar manner. As the teacher increases the volume of speech, the student's volume of speech also will increase.

Practice changing other behaviors, such as breathing, and observe similar changes in the student's behaviors. For example, if a student is speaking too rapidly, the teacher mirrors and paces that tempo. The teacher then slows the tempo of speech and observes the change in the student's tempo of speech. A comparable example might be a baby who hears the parents arguing. The baby, being too young to understand the words, yet processing the tempo, responds by crying.

A good reference for the power of pacing and leading as a method of behavior influence is the work of Janet Adler (1970). Adler was able to break the communication barrier with autistic children by mirroring and pacing their body language. This was done by entering the world of the children. Adler communicated with these children on individual levels by mirroring and pacing their body movements. When they flapped their hands, she flapped her hands. When they ran in certain ways, she ran in the same ways. Adler mirrored and paced the children as closely as possible. After pacing them for a considerable length of time, she began to lead them through the developmental stages they had missed. Soon, the children were able to respond to Adler, and to others, to accept touch and affection, to make eye contact, and, eventually, to speak.

Practice the exercises marked Level III at the end of this chapter until confidence and competence are experienced and demonstrated.

LEVEL IV: REPRESENTATIONAL SYSTEMS

The way in which a person utilizes the five physical senses affects the person's perception of the world and is a significant variable in building rapport. As a student's sensory base (visual, auditory, kinesthetic, gustatory, and olfactory) is examined, the teacher may gain an understanding of how these sensory perceptions influence the student's interpretations and representations of the world.

All of the five senses continually process information. However, most students (and people in general) have one preferred sensory modality, or avenue, through which the world is represented and interpreted. Each student's representation differs because of the way information and experiences are processed. Body movements, behavior, and language are ways in which representations of the world may be expressed. These provide strong clues to each student's preferred modality for processing information and experiences. It also gives clues to the student's strategies for thinking, for making decisions, and for relating to others.

Mirroring a student's verbal system can establish commonality and congruency with the student, thus building rapport quickly. The first step in mirroring a student's verbal system is to identify the sensory representational language system used by the student.

Human experiences are characterized in the sensory representational systems by statements such as, "I see . . . ," "I hear . . . ," and "I feel . . .". Words that indicate perceptions based on sensory interpretations also are used, e.g., "out of focus," "tune in," "a hot time," etc. Perceptions through the senses continually occur both consciously and unconsciously. These perceptions become internalized and thus govern behavior.

External behavior not only depends on the stimulus itself, but also on the sensory perception and interpretation of the stimulus. Behavior is further influenced by the person's coding or storing of interpretations within the person's language system. Bontrager (1958) stated that a person's external behavior, and the way the person expressed that behavior, were dependent upon the following variables: the intactness and nature of the organism, the nature of the stimulus, the way the organism interpreted the stimulus, and what the organism did as a result of the aforementioned. The following diagram depicts this concept:

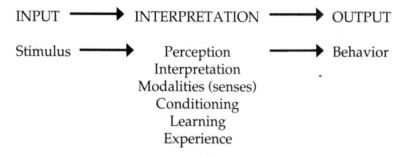

INPUT ⟶ INTERPRETATION ⟶ OUTPUT

Stimulus ⟶

Perception
Interpretation
Modalities (senses)
Conditioning
Learning
Experience

⟶ Behavior

(See Illustration 3.)

It is important to remember that each student's perception of the world is different. Paying attention to how each student represents the world is uniquely and extremely important. The type of words a student uses most often reflects the main sensory representational system being used by that student. Therefore, the teacher must concentrate on mirroring and pacing the student's sensory representational system in order to further build rapport.

How can the student's dominant sensory representational system be identified? The dominant sensory representational system in which a student is operating can be identified by listening to the predicates, verbs, adverbs, and adjectives used to describe experiences. This selection usually occurs at the student's sub-conscious level. The predicates to be sorted and categorized will fall under the following headings: 1) visual—look, see,

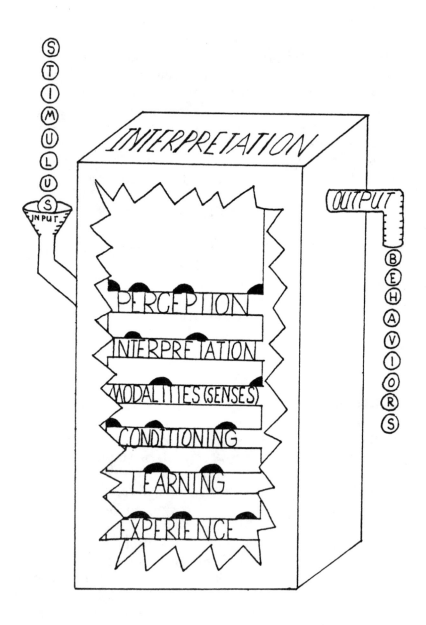

Illustration 3

picture, etc.; 2) auditory—hear, say, listen, etc.; 3) kinesthetic—feel, touch, grasp, etc.; 4) gustatory—taste, sweet, sour, etc.; and 5) olfactory—smell, odor, stink, etc. (See Appendix 2 for a list of predicate examples.)

The teacher must listen carefully to the verbs, adverbs, and adjectives that the student uses in speaking. For example, listen to the way a student ends a conversation or interaction. One student may say, "Goodbye;" another may say, "I'll be seeing you;" still another may say, "Let me hear from you," or "Call me." When a student says, "I'll be seeing you," the visual representational system is being used. "It's been nice talking to you" reflects usage of the auditory representational system. Talking, hearing, and listening connote the student's dominant functioning in the auditory representational system. If the student says, "It felt good being with you," the student is operating in the kinesthetic representational system.

Having identified the dominant or primary sensory representational system of the student, it is important that the teacher communicate with the student in the same sensory representational system in order to build rapport. If the student uses words like *look* and *see,* the teacher should use visual words in communicating with the student. By doing this, the teacher is mirroring and pacing the student's sensory representational systems. The teacher is, in effect, entering the student's world and establishing harmony and accord with the student.

When matching the student's predicates, the teacher is mirroring the student and building rapport, which often leads to cooperation and motivation for learning. For example: A teacher writes a note on the student's project report, "I don't see evidence of documentation for your conclusion." The student talks to the teacher after class and says, "I can tell you must have missed the documentation I included (or thought I included), but I'd like to explain to you what I said." The teacher answers, "I must see it in writing, so if you'd like to write an additional paragraph and give it to me tomorrow, that would be fine." The student complains to other students that the teacher does not understand and is creating unnecessary extra work. The teacher assumes the position of being kind and lenient in allowing the student to add to the report.

The student is operating in the auditory representational system, as evidenced by the use of the predicates *tell* and *said*. The teacher is operating in the visual representational system, as evidenced by the use of the predicate *see*.

In terms of enhancing communication, cooperation, and mutual understanding, it would benefit both teacher and student to have the flexibility of matching each other's sensory representational systems. In particular, the teacher may realize that the student's preferred sensory representational system is auditory and that the student may be less able to reflect ideas in writing. The teacher may then agree to listen to what the student has to say in further explaining the report. The teacher would have a better understanding of the student's report. The student's level of motivation would be elevated, and both would experience a sense of cooperation.

Another example occurred when one of the authors was supervising a group of student teachers. While visiting a particular classroom, he observed the student teacher presenting a lesson in geography. The student teacher used many maps and visual displays to explain where Brazil is located in relation to the United States. One student raised his hand many times, explaining to the teacher each time that he did not "grasp" how Brazil could be to the south of the United States. Each time the student teacher explained it to the student, she pointed to the map, showing the location; and each time, the student seemed to have a puzzled look on his face. Finally, the author walked over to the boy, pointed the boy's arm down (south) and said, "Brazil is down here, south of the United States. Feel the United States being north as your arm goes up. Feel Brazil being south as your arm goes down." The student turned to the author, smiled, and said, "That feels right."

In another setting, one of the authors observed a teacher helping a student learn how to spell phonetically. The instructions were as follows: "Sound out each syllable of the word 'phonics'." Each time, the student complied and wrote on the board "F O N I C S". The teacher repeated the directions, "Sound out the word 'phonics'." The student replied, "It doesn't look right, but that's the way it sounds."

The teacher gave the instructions in an auditory representational system, to which the student correctly responded. However, the teacher's intention was to have the student correctly spell, in writing, the word "phonics". The student was aware that in spelling "phonics" as it sounded, the word "FONICS" looked wrong and sounded right. The teacher's instructions did not clearly reflect the task. The teacher also did not realize that the word "phonics," like many other English words, are difficult to spell correctly when using an auditory representational system.

In each of these examples, the teacher did not notice or utilize the student's preferred sensory representational system as an aid to effective teaching. When the sensory representational system being reflected by the student is observed by the teacher, clues indicating how the student is processing information are evident. The teacher can utilize these clues to increase the student's basic understanding, task accomplishment, and learning processes.

Practice the activity for Level IV at the end of this chapter until confidence and competence are experienced at this level. This exercise will further develop skills in matching and pacing a student's sensory representational system.

LEVEL V: BECOMING SENSITIVE TO A STUDENT'S FEEDBACK

Rapport is a two-way street. While mirroring and pacing are important, it is imperative that the teacher observe the student's reactions to the teacher's own physical and verbal behavior. For example, one of the authors lectured in a small southern community. Near the beginning of the lecture, profanity was used to illustrate the language of a particular child in a treatment center. Many of the people in the audience quickly began to display changes in body movements and breathing rates, some shaking their heads in a side to side motion. The audience as a whole withdrew into silence. Even though this profanity had been used as an example of a treatment situation, rapport had been broken. The lecturer had to reestablish rapport. The lecture evaluation indicated that 90% of the audience mentioned the use of profanity. This illustrates how one must be sensitive to the sensory representational systems of both individuals and groups.

In order to increase awareness of sensory activity, think of situations in which material has been presented (by you or to you) involving a large group; then think about the sensory cues which were present and which may have indicated acceptance/non-acceptance and/or understanding/lack of understanding of the material presented. Were there signs, such as body shifting (movement), heads shaking up and down or side to side, or sighs of heavy breathing? Did the lecturer indicate an awareness and sensitivity to this understanding, lack of understanding, or restlessness? Was there a change in content, tempo, or method of delivery, or perhaps a premature or unplanned break?

In presenting material, the teacher must be sensitive to the dominant, and possibly changing, sensory representational system of the student. A teacher may initially present material in one's own preferred sensory representational system. If the material is not understood or learned by the student, the teacher then may wish to present the material in the student's preferred representational system. The teacher also should observe feedback. The teacher must be sensitive to, and adjust to, the sensory mode, language, behavior, tempo, method of delivery, and amount of content, etc. of the particular student, group, and/or situation. The teacher must develop sensitivity to all sensory representational systems, use feedback, and modify behavior and language in order to be in harmony and communication with a student or group of students. Also, establishing such rapport may reduce the time and energy expended to impart the information and expedite learning.

LEVEL VI: CALIBRATION

Calibration is the next level in developing rapport. Calibration is the ability to see or hear something a student does and then match or associate it with a particular internal state. (See Illustration 4.) For example, the teacher observes that a student's body tempo and skin color have changed from what they are normally. These changes occur when the student is ill. By matching the appearance of these changes and conditions with the student

CALIBRATING RESPONSES ENABLE YOU TO KNOW
AN INDIVIDUAL'S INTERNAL STATE, FEELINGS, ETC.
BY READING HIS EXTERNAL BEHAVIORS.

Illustration 4

being ill, the teacher has developed the ability to calibrate an external behavior with an internal state. This calibration or association of two or more conditions may be generalized to other students, as well as teachers and other adults.

To further illustrate calibration: The teacher observes that a student says "yes " and nods the head in an up and down motion. By observing the association of these two behaviors over a period of time, the teacher knows that when the student's head moves in an up and down motion, it is congruent with a "yes" response. However, if the student is asked a question to which the verbal response is "no," but the student's head moves in an up and down motion, the teacher may wish to explore the situation further, based on incongruency with the teacher's past calibrations. By reading external behaviors and calibrating responses, the teacher will gain a better understanding of the student's true functioning, feelings, and possibly even the student's internal state of being. Body movements and body language are usually more accurate indicators of what is true, rather than verbal expressions (Merabian, 1972).

Practice the exercises in Level VI to refine observation, sensory acuity, and calibration skills until confidence and competence are experienced and demonstrated consistently.

NOTE: In each of the exercises, the participants should switch roles for more variety and practice. The student's role is to be played by an adult.

LEVEL I

EXERCISE: MIRRORING
PURPOSE: To improve skills in observing and mirroring. To improve skills in matching body changes.
ROLES: Teacher, Student (played by an adult), Consultant
DIRECTIONS: T and S face each other. T mirrors and matches S. C stands behind S, facing and observing T. S is directed to talk about two specific experiences that resulted in different emotional responses e.g., a successful lesson, winning a sports event, an award, etc. For example, while S is describing experience #1 and displaying excitement, T mirrors the behaviors and expres-

sions of S. While S is describing experience #2 and displaying embarrassment, T then mirrors the behaviors and expressions of S. S then selects one of the two experiences and re-creates it. While S is again describing it, T mirrors the behaviors and expressions of S. C then must determine which experience S is expressing.

LEVEL I

EXERCISE: BUILDING RAPPORT
PURPOSE: To improve skills in observing the different movements which students may demonstrate while engaged in conversation. To match movements in order to maintain rapport.
ROLES: Teacher, Student
DIRECTIONS: T and S face each other and begin talking. T observes S, particularly noting body language, breathing, voice tempo, and voice tone. T begins to mirror or match S's movements. T continues to match S's behaviors, expressions, and movements, so that rapport is not broken. It may be necessary for T to pause before matching S's movements with the same part of T 's body.

LEVEL II

EXERCISE: MATCHING AND MISMATCHING
PURPOSE: To increase perceptual skills. To develop flexibility in matching skills. To develop flexibility in mismatching skills.
ROLES: Teacher, Student, Consultant
DIRECTIONS: S is asked to leave the room. Prior to S's return, T is instructed to talk to, but mismatch S. C is instructed to match S's breathing. Upon returning to the room, S and T begin a conversation for an allotted time (3-5 minutes). At the end of this time, T and S share observations of what they experienced.
   NOTE: Observe that when rapport with S has been gained through matched breathing (by C), S frequently begins to direct most conversation to C rather than to T.

LEVEL II

EXERCISE: BUILDING RAPPORT II—
CROSS-OVER MIRRORING
PURPOSE: To improve skills in observing, pacing and cross-over mirroring.
ROLES: Teacher, Student
DIRECTIONS: T and S face each other and engage in a conversation. T mirrors and paces S's behaviors, using cross-over mirroring. For example, this can be done by having T pace S's breathing with swinging foot, hand, or arm movement, by a rocking movement of the body, or by voice tempo. After T has established rapport with cross-over mirroring, the participants should reverse roles.

LEVEL III

EXERCISE: BUILDING RAPPORT—
PACING AND LEADING
PURPOSE: To further build and improve skills in building rapport, pacing and leading.
ROLES: Teacher, Student, Consultant
DIRECTIONS: Rapport is established by T, who is conversing with S. For a short period of time, T breaks rapport with S by mismatching. T then reestablishes rapport with S. Observations are described by C.

Calibration skills may be exercised by allowing S and T to discuss their internal feelings and thoughts.

LEVEL III

EXERCISE: BUILDING RAPPORT—
PACING AND LEADING
PURPOSE: To improve skills in building rapport and pacing.
ROLES: Teacher, Student, Consultant
DIRECTIONS: T and S begin by discussing a disappointing experience. T should pace S with breathing, body movements, facial expressions, eye movements, eye blinks, voice tempo,

posture, idiosyncratic movements, etc. T should use at least one cross-over mirroring technique. T must change one of the above rapport building behaviors after rapport has been established. If S follows T's lead, increased rapport is established.

C observes and reports feedback in sensory-specific language. For example: You paced the Student's breathing with your hand and cross-paced the Student's head nods by moving your foot.

LEVEL IV

EXERCISE: REPRESENTATIONAL SYSTEMS AND PREDICATES
PURPOSE: To recognize the representational systems of students as indicated by predicates in both oral and written work.
ROLES: Teacher, Student
DIRECTIONS: S is instructed to discuss what she would do for our country if given one million dollars. T records specific predicates that S uses.

T requests that S write an essay on the same subject. Again, T records specific predicates that are written by S.

T compares the predicates used in both oral and written exercises.
CONTINUATION: Code the predicates by using the following system:

1) A = Auditory
2) V = Visual
3) K = Kinesthetic
4) G = Gustatory
5) O = Olfactory

LEVEL V

EXERCISE: BUILDING SENSORY OBSERVATION SKILLS
PURPOSE: To increase skills in observation and response to sensory feedback. To increase perceptual skills.
ROLES: Teacher, Student, Consultant/Observer

DIRECTIONS: T interacts with S. C observes and records the varying sensory responses of both T and S.

C notes any changes in T 's presentation as a result of feedback given by S.

CONTINUATION: Note and record if T modifies predicate usage to improve communication.

LEVEL V

EXERCISE: BUILDING SENSORY SKILLS
PURPOSE: To further develop calibration skills based on sensory data.
ROLES: Teacher, Student, Observer/Verifier
DIRECTIONS: T describes S in sensory-based terms. O is instructed to interrupt T (at any time) when sensory-based terms are not being used. Sensory-based descriptions must be objective observations, rather than inferences or interpretations.

For example: Acceptable observations include 1) Your eyes are closed; 2) You moved your right hand; 3) You coughed twice in 30 seconds. Unacceptable observation statements include l) Your eyes are sad; 2) Your hand moved because you are nervous; 3) You look relaxed.

LEVEL VI

EXERCISE: CALIBRATION
PURPOSE: To develop calibration skills based on sensory data.
ROLES: Teacher, Student
DIRECTIONS: T asks S a series of Yes/No questions. For example: Is your hair black? Are you a student? Are you in Florida? etc. T watches S's eye and body responses while S answers Yes or No.

S is asked another series of Yes/No questions, and is instructed to lie when giving some of the responses. T observes the sensory cues of S to determine whether or not S is lying about specific questions.

Chapter 2
Understanding And Programming States of Learning

ADVANCED ORGANIZER

OVERVIEW

In this chapter, you will be provided with a series of techniques which will enable you to understand how individual students develop states of learning that both enhance and retard learning. The techniques for anchoring, establishing magic buttons, stacking anchors, and chaining anchors will be presented and elaborated upon with implications for education.

Anchoring is a conditioning technique that will provide you with a broad and generic framework in which you will be able to identify where, when, and how specific interferences to learning occur and how they are maintained. The technique for establishing "magic buttons" will be explained and examples will be given for its use in reducing negative, interfering associations. Procedures for chaining and stacking anchors will be presented. Their potential for use in dealing with hyperactivity will be explored.

CONCEPTS

Anchoring—The process by which an external stimulus is paired with an internal state (similar to classical conditioning). When the external stimulus is presented, the internal state is elicited. For example, when you are driving fast and you hear the loud siren of a police car, you develop an internal state of rapid heart beats and increased respiration. It is highly probable that the same or a similar stimulus would bring about the same response at another time. Anchors may be established in any representational system—auditory, visual, kinesthetic, olfactory, or gustatory. They may serve to control both positive and negative internal states.

Magic Buttons—Pre-established anchors for positive states. For example, a person may be guided to recreate a pleasant, relaxed experience with the same feelings of calmness and confidence originally felt. These feelings may then be anchored by pressing a special spot on the body. This kinesthetic anchor or "magic button" then may be used by the person to recreate the positive internal feelings whenever desired or needed.

Chaining Anchors—A procedure by which a series of anchors are established. Each link in the chain represents an anchor for a specific response. The chain is built to start from one state and lead through a series of states until the desired state is reached. For example, a teacher may work with a student and establish the following kinesthetic anchors. Pressure of the first knuckle of the student's right hand recreates the feelings of anxiety associated with tests. Pressure on the second knuckle may be the anchor associated with a past calm, relaxed state. Pressure on the third knuckle results in the reexperiencing of a time when the student was confident and successful. By pressing the knuckles in sequence, the teacher can set off a chain of responses. These may be described as follows: Anxiety—Calmness—Confidence. When triggered by future test-related anxiety situations, the student can be returned to a calm state by the teacher or student 'firing" the chain of anchors.

Stacking Anchors—The utilization of a series of events associated with one specific anchor. These procedures strengthen the intensity of a subject's response to a specific anchor. For example, if the teacher has the student relive a number of positive experiences dealing with relaxation and anchors each experience in the same manner, the overall effect will be much more powerful.

VOCABULARY

Conditioning—When a stimulus be comes paired with a specific response. A process by which specific stimuli come to control specific responses.

Future Pacing—Projecting oneself into a future situation in which a stimulus triggers an internal response that elicits a specific behavior. Future pacing allows the changes accomplished during therapy or an educational session to become generalized to other contexts or situations. The primary method of future pacing entails installing new behaviors or resources for the future.

Hyperactivity—Purposeless movements.

States of Learning—A mental and emotional set which facilitates learning.

UNDERSTANDING AND PROGRAMMING STATES OF LEARNING

THE PROCESS OF ANCHORING

Anchoring is a process in which an external stimulus becomes paired with an internal state. When the original or similar external stimulus reoccurs, the resultant internal state will be produced again. This internal state can be productive or counterproductive.

For example, think about driving down the road and seeing a stop sign. What happens internally? Perhaps you feel your right foot begin to move toward the brake, or perhaps you see an internal picture of a car stopping, or you hear a voice saying, "Stop!" Any or all of these internal responses have been associated to the stimulus of the stop sign so that you no longer "have to think" about what to do. It just happens. This process of association between the external stimulus and the internal response is what is referred to as anchoring in Neuro Linguistic Programming.

"MAGIC BUTTONS"

As an educator or future educator, you may be asking yourself questions on how to structure an environment for learning. You then may think about bright and airy classrooms and materials for optimum learning experiences. While it is true that the external environment plays an important part in setting the stage for much learning, it is the internal environment of the person and the person's use of it that is most influential in learning. Although external environmental factors for learning are important, internal environmental factors make the critical difference in learning.

The first step in understanding an individual's internal environment is to understand the concept of anchoring. Anchoring will provide your students with a conditional response ("magic button") that can be utilized to trigger desirable internal states of learning.

Think of a time when you learned something in a pleasant, comfortable manner (academically or otherwise). Once you have isolated that experience, allow yourself to step into the experience by seeing what you see, hearing what you hear, and feeling what you feel. Be sure that, as you review the memory, you step into the experience and into your own body, and that you are actually seeing, hearing, and feeling the events from within yourself. In other words, you are seeing them as you saw them, hearing them as you heard them, and feeling them as you felt them at that time. You will reexperience the sensations and feelings that you had at that time. This process is also referred to as *revivification*.

As you reexperience the feelings of pleasantness and comfortable feelings, squeeze any two fingers together. After five seconds, release your fingers. Now allow a minute to pass, then lightly squeeze the same two fingers again, using the same amount of pressure. Pay attention to how the same feelings of pleasantness and comfort return. The squeezing of two fingers has become associated or paired with a set of internal feelings. This happened because you paired or conditioned the squeezing of two fingers with those feelings. These feelings of pleasantness and comfort may provide an internal state which is conducive to learning. The authors have used this technique with children and have labeled it "magic buttons."

"Magic buttons" may be illustrated further with the following experience. A ten year old student was frightened by authority figures. When the principal entered the classroom, the student began to shake. The teacher was taught by one of the authors the technique of "magic buttons" to develop a state of calmness and confidence in the student. The following is what happened.

The teacher instructed the student to go back in time to an experience when the student felt calm and confident. The student recalled an experience when she went camping with her father. She remembered being anxious about having the responsibility for the evening meal. After cooking the meal, her father complemented her on her ability to prepare a quality meal under such primitive circumstances. She then recalled the calm and confident feeling she had as she sat by the campfire and planned the next day's evening meal.

The teacher observed the student as she proceeded through the experience, suggesting to the student that she nod her head slightly when she was really experiencing the specific past event. When the student nodded her head, the teacher told the student to stay there (at that point in the experience). The teacher then squeezed the student's left wrist gently and held it for five seconds. The teacher released the student's wrist and, after five seconds, the teacher clapped her hands to distract the student. (This was done to break the internal state that the student was reliving.) The teacher again touched the student's wrist and observed her. This was done to see if it would bring back the same internal state. The teacher noted the same physical changes, such as relaxation, etc., that occurred when the student was accessing or experiencing the camping event. The teacher then released the student's wrist.

To confirm that anchoring had taken place, the teacher asked the student if the touch brought back the same feelings of confidence and sense of calmness as felt in the camping experience with her father. She responded, "Yes, it did!" The teacher then taught the student to squeeze her wrist in exactly the same place, with exactly the same pressure, when the student felt the need for such a resource. The teacher then arranged for the principal to visit the classroom. When the principal entered the room, the student followed the teacher's instructions and touched her wrist in the same spot the teacher had touched. She immediately felt calm and confident in the presence of the principal.

It is important to realize that anchoring may be effective in many anxiety states. In this particular example, the student was able to retrieve the resource of calmness and confidence that occurred in the context of the camping trip. This feeling then was associated through anchoring or "magic buttons" within the context of the classroom and the principal. This calm, confident state neutralized the anxiety state which was associated previously with the principal. The student was delighted with this newly found resource. The student continued to utilize this resource when confronted with situations that previously evoked the anxiety state. It was even useful in taking a test in arithmetic the following day.

STEPS IN ANCHORING

The sequence of steps to be used in the anchoring process is outlined below. As you use anchoring more and more, you will learn to use it in a natural, unobtrusive way. For now, follow the procedure described below:

1. Establish and maintain rapport with the student.
2. Ask the student to find a context or situation in which positive or good feelings such as joy, happiness, acceptance, success, etc., are or were felt.
3. Ask the student to relive that time or scene, and experience it in full detail by visualizing the experience. Tell the student to step inside his/her body and actually be there. Then instruct the student, "See what you see, hear what you hear, and feel what you feel. When you are really experiencing the event, slightly move your little finger and remain in the experience." (When doing this, use present tense verbs.)
4. When the teacher sees the student move the little finger, the teacher touches a "magic spot" (wrist, earlobe, etc.) and holds that spot for five seconds. The teacher then releases the touch. It is important that the spot selected be both convenient and

easily accessible to the student. This specific spot ultimately becomes the student's "magic button."

5. To test the anchor, have the student again touch the "magic button" to verify that it brings forth the same feelings. If the same positive feelings as experienced previously do not reoccur, repeat the above steps. Check to make sure you are touching the same spot with the same amount of pressure.

Anchoring is a universal process that pairs together an external stimulus with an internal state. The teacher can thus understand how learning can randomly and unknowingly be anchored in a number of different states. Some of these states can enhance learning, whereas other states can interfere with learning.

Anchoring may also be related to the place (chair, desk, etc.) in which a student sits. Try moving a student from a seat/area where frequent failure has been experienced to another seat/area. Observe the student to determine if there is a difference. It is possible for one chair to be an anchor for failure and another to be an anchor for success. The failure chair may be nullified by moving the student to another chair/area.

Perhaps you have seen some students who have resented certain teachers with common physical characteristics, even though their personalities were very different. Usually, there has been a visual anchor that has been established or conditioned. At some point, this visual anchor has been associated with an unpleasant or negative experience. It is important that the teacher recognize this situation, find the anchor, and help the student to change it.

Knowing that anchors and stimulus response chains can occur on a random basis explains two things: first, it provides an explanation of how numerous difficulties in learning situations may occur; secondly, using anchoring as a framework, the teacher can observe and determine the problem, implement change, and control anchors that interfere with optimal learning. By observing a student, asking questions, isolating the problem and anchors, the teacher can use the anchoring process to create desirable changes in the student. For example, if the teacher's voice is raised a certain way in a classroom and a particular student repeatedly gets upset and hostile, the assumption can be made that there is an anchored response between the voice tone or volume of the teacher and the student's emotional state.

For many students, behavioral problems are the result of anchoring being manifested and reinforced over periods of time. Anchoring can often explain and also correct the constant manifestation of many behavioral problems. The student who is disruptive and belligerent every time the student is touched by the teacher or another student may well have associated touch with being hit or punished. If so, the student's internal response of fear is triggered each time the teacher's hand appears to move toward the student. The student thus becomes defensive by being disruptive, argumentative, or aggressive. The teacher very quickly learns that any attempt to touch the student results in a negative response. The teacher adeptly learns not to touch the student, or neutralizes that anchor with another anchor. This will be further explained in Chapter 4.

Another common example of anchoring in the classroom occurs with the "sensitive student." A particular student is commonly known as being bright and intelligent. For some unknown reason, the student becomes very quiet and withdrawn in the classroom of a particular teacher.

In several cases of "sensitive students," the authors have found that when the teacher speaks in a specific tonality or volume, the student associates that specific tonality or volume with some unpleasant experience in the home or some other place or experience. This tonality or volume has been anchored to a negative set of feelings in the student. When the student hears the stimulus, the tonality and/or volume of the teacher's voice, the anchored internal negative experience is triggered from the past, resulting in the "quiet student" and withdrawal behavior.

This same phenomenon may also occur when certain facial expressions are displayed by teachers. Certain students may react to a negative anchor when a particular teacher creates a specific facial expression. This may occur with or without the teacher's or student's awareness.

For example, consider a student who has had successful experiences taking tests. That same student fails a test for some unknown reason. The teacher quite severely reprimands the student for failing that test. When the parents are informed by the student of the failure to pass the test, the parents also severely reprimand the student.

The next time the student takes a test, this situation is relived in the mind and the chastisement by both the teacher and parents is vividly remembered. The student's muscles become tense and anxiety increases tremendously. As the teacher gives the student a copy of the test, the student perceives the teacher to be giving a stern look similar to the one given at the time of the previous test failure. The student's anxiety and tension increase even more. This is an example of visual anchoring. The teacher also remarks to the student in the same harsh tone of voice used previously that the student better do well on this test. This is an example of auditory anchoring and further reinforces the student's anxiety. This stern look and harsh tone of voice, both of which were used previously in the teacher's reprimand, now elicit the same anxious responses the student experienced when he first heard the harsh tone and saw the stern look. The student has now become so anxious that the anxiety state interferes with the student's current performance. As a result, the student fails the test.

Thus, a vicious cycle of negative anchoring is now in operation. If the teacher continues to reprimand and to present to this student a stern look and harsh tone of voice before and after tests, the student will probably continue to perform far below true performance or optimum level. This has occurred because of the negative internal state that has been triggered by test-taking. Several anchors or associations have been added to the original stimulus. Thereafter, every time the student observes the teacher using the same stern look or the same harsh tone of voice, these factors become negative anchors that will elicit anxiety in the student, which may be counterproductive.

Teachers must become aware of this process so that the installing of negative anchors in students can be avoided. Even more important, students must be taught how to undo, change, or reverse negative anchors and the resultant negative states.

In understanding some of the rudiments of anchoring, the teacher may ask, "What do they want from us—robots?" The answer to this question is "No." A robot-like teacher would still trigger anchors in students, even if the voice, tonality, and volume were never modulated, facial expressions never changed, and students were never specifically related to by teachers. In fact, it would be best that the teacher become the opposite of a robot.

The authors suggest that you, the teacher, observe yourself and each student, and that you vary your voice tonality, your touch, and facial expressions. Observe the responses in the students with whom you are communicating and teaching. This will provide you with a way to calibrate or to match the stimuli that you offer to the paired responses of the student. Being able to calibrate responses enables the teacher to observe what is done and the response(s) produced. Thus, you can now install positive states of learning. Having reached this point, you are now beginning the process of excellence in teaching.

HYPERACTIVITY AND ANCHORING

"If only they would keep still, we could get some work done!" is a cry heard frequently in today's classrooms. Of all the problems facing teachers in their daily quests to instill specific learning outcomes in students, hyperactivity is considered a frequent and common obstruction to optimal learning.

The definition of hyperactivity (in terms of education) presents difficulty and confusion, because what is hyperactivity to one teacher is "youthful enthusiasm" to another teacher. The appropriate level of activity for a specific learning experience for one teacher may be too little or too much for another teacher. However, it is neither necessary nor desirable to determine an operational definition of hyperactivity that would be acceptable to a majority of teachers. For the purpose of this book, the definition of hyperactivity is determined by the specific frame of reference of the reader. (We generally agree that hyperactivity is continued, purposeless movement.)

It is important that both teachers and students accept a reciprocal responsibility for recognition of individual differences. Thus, if a teacher feels that a certain level of activity exceeds the threshold of acceptance, that level, in effect, is the level that students must not cross in that teacher's classroom. Expectations and standards of activity will vary above and below a mean level of activity, resulting in overcontrol by teachers in some classrooms and permissiveness in other classrooms.

In essence, it is the responsibility of each teacher to set the limits of acceptable activity level in a particular classroom, then to convey these limits to the students. Teachers and administrators may wish to jointly develop common, but wide, limits of acceptable activity levels. However, teachers must maintain balance and flexibility in their own classrooms. In turn, students will benefit from learning to adjust to a variety of activity levels within certain stated limits.

Anchoring can serve to both increase and decrease levels of activity in specific students. The teacher may discover that associations have been established unknowingly, thus anchoring the very behavior intended for extinction. For example, the days just prior to major holidays may reflect associations and anchors for increased movement and talking. Entire student populations in schools have been known to become overly active just prior to Christmas. The sights, sounds, and smells of Christmas are anchors that have been associated with a wide variety of behaviors. School situations change; certain previously prohibited behaviors are allowed because "It's Christmas." It is understandable that students may test the limits of acceptable activity levels and that numerous anchors may be presented, thus causing more problems than usual.

At other times, just the opposite may occur. For example, the time just prior to an exam or report card distribution is characterized by a marked decrease in movement and taking. The associations with tests and report cards constitute a different set of anchors and result in a lower activity level. It appears that, regardless of individual definitions of hyperactivity and of activity levels, these activities and changes follow the same principles of anchoring.

There are times when a combination of associations may serve to heighten the effects of anchoring. For example, imagine the feelings of enthusiasm and even hyperactive behavior elicited while viewing a particular sport or entertainment event. The roar of the crowd (auditory), combined with the observation of the event (visual) and the sensory-motor expressions of school loyalty (kinesthetic), may well result in even the most placid of individuals of any age behaving like enthusiastic teenagers at a rock concert.

When dealing with hyperactivity in a learning situation, anchors become doubly important. First, the anchors may be an intrinsic part of the behavior itself. A student running about a classroom may become frenzied by the self-stimulation of the activity. The activity itself serves to anchor even more activity. The behavior thus becomes self-maintaining. Secondly, the environmental response to hyperactivity may also serve as an anchor, because its association serves to trigger and maintain the behavior.

For example, if a student is constantly out of the assigned seat and running about the room, that behavior is accompanied by repeated kinesthetic contacts, visual displays, and auditory input from the teacher and other students. The overwhelming complexity of such an atmosphere makes it very difficult to isolate individual anchors. It is most likely that the behavior is heightened by the stacking of anchor upon anchor in all sensory representational systems. Therefore, it is beneficial to systematically isolate those anchors, so that they can be individually utilized by the teacher in effecting classroom control. (Teachers have found cubicles to be a viable way of reducing hyperactive behavior in certain students. The cubicle reduces the exposure of potential anchors that could set off the student.)

When the teacher observes the student in a calm state, the teacher should anchor (visually, auditorally, and kinesthetically if possible) that state in the student. Usually, extremely hyperactive students require many such pairings. (Be sure to use the same anchoring procedure each time you anchor the calmness state.)

When you see the student beginning to display hyperactivity, fire the preestablished calmness anchors and watch the effect on the student's behavior.

CHAINING ANCHORS

The technique described above is effective in reducing hyper-activity; however, there is an advanced strategy that is also useful in this treatment. In the advanced strategy, the teacher works with the student to develop a chain of anchors. These new anchors are self-established and situationally triggered. With this technique, hyperactive students are assisted in developing a strategy for productivity as well as for calmness.

These new responses will occur in a provoking situation, or even when only the "internal cue" for hyperactivity occurs. By training the student in a new sequence and rehearsing it again and again, the behavior soon becomes part of a new chain. This new chain is then elicited when the original anchor is triggered. This is similar to the adage of "count to ten" when faced with an anger-producing situation. The teacher's specific role in establishing this chain of new anchors, corresponding associated states, and the student's new set of behaviors (which replace hyperactivity) will now be described. The steps are as follows:

STEP 1

When a chronic state of hyperactivity or maladaptive behaviors occurs, the teacher meets privately with the student as soon as possible. The teacher describes the specific maladaptive behavior concisely. In doing so, the behavior must be stated so explicitly that either the student or the teacher could imitate it. It is also important for the teacher to establish and maintain rapport with the student.

STEP 2

After the hyperactive or maladaptive behavior is identified specifically, the teacher guides the student in determining and describing a more appropriate behavior or response that is mutually acceptable and desirable to both the teacher and student. In doing this, the teacher and student establish a new behavior objective, toward which both are working, e.g., quiet productivity. Remember: It is important that the new behavior be mutually identified, clearly described, and understood by both the teacher and student.

STEP 3

Now that both desirable and undesirable behavior have been identified by both the teacher and student, the chain can be completed. At this point, the student is asked to add in the step or steps that are necessary in order to proceed from the original behavior (LEVEL A) to the desired behavior (LEVEL C). This may be illustrated as follows:

LEVEL A	LEVEL B	LEVEL C
Hyper-activity	Connecting steps, as determined by student, assisted by teacher	Quiet produc-tivity

With the teacher's assistance, LEVEL B is then identified by the student. For purposes of illustration, both teacher and student agree that a calm, relaxed state is the desired connecting step and a good resource state. If this is the resource state used previously, the completed chain is illustrated as follows:

LEVEL A	LEVEL B	LEVEL C
Hyper-activity	Calm and relaxed	Quiet produc-tivity

STEP 4

Given the mutually identified and accepted sequence outlined above, the teacher is ready to begin anchoring the new chain. It is important to stress again the necessity of the teacher maintaining rapport with the student during the next steps.

First, the student is asked to relive the experience labeled "hyperactivity." As the student relives the experience, the teacher says, "Step inside your body and see what you see, hear what you hear, and feel what you feel. When you are really experiencing the event, move your little finger." As the student is reliving the seeing, hearing, and feeling parts of the experience, the teacher presses on the first knuckle of the student's right hand (or any other appropriate anchoring spot). This pressure serves as a kinesthetic anchor for the hyperactive state.

After the hyperactive state is anchored, the teacher checks to see if the anchor is set. To do this, the teacher presses the student's first knuckle on the right hand and asks the student to report on the experience. If the student reports the recreation of the hyper-activity state (the original association), the anchor is set.

In addition to the student's verbal report, the teacher observes other physical changes. These changes may include changes in breathing, posture shifts, facial colorations, or facial expressions. Observing such behaviors and identifying them with given states provides the teacher with additional information. The teacher may then match specific behaviors observed when the anchor spot is pressed.

STEP 5

With the hyperactivity anchor established on the first knuckle of the right hand (tested and confirmed), the teacher is ready for LEVEL B of the chain—the resource state of being calm and relaxed. The student is instructed to think of a time in her life when she experienced a state of relaxation and calmness. The student is instructed to relive the experience of relaxation and calmness. As the student reexperiences the situation, the teacher again repeats, "Step into your body as if you were there, and see what you see, hear what you hear, and feel what you feel." At the same time that the student is reliving the experience, the teacher presses on the second knuckle of the student's right hand. This anchor is then tested to assure its establishment or set.

STEP 6

The same procedure outlined above is used with the final state of "quiet productivity" (LEVEL C). The teacher insures that the behaviors the student reexperiences are compatible with quiet productivity, and again anchors the response, using the third knuckle on the student's right hand. Again, test the anchor.

STEP 7

After anchoring the three levels in the chain, the teacher adds a fourth level—requesting the student to look into the future. The student identifies a time or situation in which the student may need to use the new chain. When the student identifies such a situation, the teacher instructs the student to reexperience the quiet productive state. When this is accomplished, the teacher presses the fourth knuckle of the student's right hand. This technique of future pacing serves to complete the chain.

STEP 8

Having established all anchors, the teacher now triggers each anchor sequentially by pressing (in order) the first knuckle, the second knuckle, the third knuckle, and the fourth knuckle on the student's right hand. The student will experience the sensation of going from one state to the next in a smooth transition. The teacher must be careful to trigger the anchors in sequence. Triggering any two states simultaneously will collapse one of the anchor states. Chaining is a transition "from—to," rather than a collapse. The teacher repeats the sequence four times, each time a little faster than the previous time. In addition, as the teacher presses the knuckle of the student, the "state" is verbalized.

For example, when the teacher presses the second knuckle, "calm, relaxed state" is verbalized. When the teacher touches the third knuckle, "quiet productivity" is verbalized, and in touching the fourth knuckle, "quiet productivity" is verbalized again. When the teacher presses the fourth knuckle, it is held slightly longer with each repeated sequence. This adds auditory to kinesthetic anchors and proves to more effective.

For additional effect, the student may be instructed to set the anchors on the right hand with the student's left hand. The process is repeated, with the student setting the anchors. This can be done with the student repeating each state and setting an anchor on each knuckle, or having the teacher put a finger over the student's finger and repeat the steps.

When the original behavior occurs in the classroom, the student is instructed to press the calm button—calm knuckle. This will bring forth the desirable internal state. The above technique has an extensive variety of applications. As it is used and proficiency is gained, a wider range of applications will become apparent.

EXERCISE 1: ANCHORING CONFIDENCE

PURPOSE: To give the teacher the resource of a "confidence anchor" to use with students.

ROLES: Teacher, Student

DIRECTIONS: T observes S in situations that indicate confidence, such as a game situation, talking with friends, or receiving a good grade on a test.

T uses observations from above situations to select sensory information which indicates a high level of confidence. At the moment of the highest level of confidence, T places a hand on S's shoulder and exerts slight pressure. T repeats this anchoring action at least three times, thus stacking anchor on anchor. This establishes a strong resource state of confidence.

In the future, when S falters or experiences difficulty, T uses the confidence anchor and triggers it by exerting the same pressure as before on the same spot.

EXERCISE 2: ANCHORING YOURSELF

PURPOSE: To establish a calm state within yourself. To redirect yourself to a confident state.

ROLES: Teacher

DIRECTIONS: Identify a situation in which you felt calm and/or confident. Imagine yourself as being in the experience now, feeling calm and/or confident.

When you see, hear, and feel the experience, anchor it by touching yourself in a specific spot with a specific pressure. Release it briefly, then touch the same anchor spot again. If you again imagined the experience and the feelings of calmness and confidence, you have successfully anchored yourself.

Continue to "stack" positive experiences, anchoring each in the same manner as the above.

Test the anchor when you desire or need a calming influence.

Chapter 3
Diagnostic Map of
Representational Sorts:
How The Mind Works

ADVANCED ORGANIZER

OVERVIEW

In this chapter, a model will be presented that will enable you to understand how past memories can trigger emotional states.

The first mode is called association. In this memory mode, the mind associates certain states that may be positive or negative. In the positive associative mode, the mind relives past experiences of pleasant associations. In the negative associative mode, the mind remembers and relives past negative experiences. For example, if you have experienced an unpleasant event at your place of work, you will probably continue to think about it when you go home, and will relive it several times. The emphasis and repetition will vary, depending upon the individual.

The second mode is called disassociation. In this memory mode, the mind disassociates positive or negative memories. In this mode, the individual will think about the experiences, but the feelings will be reduced or eliminated when remembering the events of a day. These processes can be productive or counterproductive, depending upon the context of the situation. The teacher's task is to create internal states which are conducive to optimal learning.

CONCEPTS

Positive Mode of Association—The state in which individuals recreate feelings connected with a past event which is positive in nature. For example, a positive mode of association would result in the warm, proud feeling a mother would have when remembering something special that one of her children accomplished.

Positive Mode of Disassociation—The state in which an individual reviews a pleasant experience. In the recreation, the scene is reviewed from the perspective of an outside observer. Thus, the intensity of the feelings is reduced. For example, when a person remembers a happy occasion, it is as if the person were watching a pleasant personal experience on a movie screen. From this perspective, disassociation results in diminished feelings.

Negative Mode of Association—The state in which an individual recreates a memory as if it were actually being experienced. The negative feelings of the past event are relived. For example, an individual who remembers being mugged records that experience/memory in the negative associative mode. The individual will relive the feelings as if the experience were happening again.

Negative Mode of Disassociation—The state in which an individual recreates a negative memory as if it were seen on a movie screen. Feelings about the scene are disassociated. In the mugging example, the individual who recreates the memory on the movie screen will have disassociated feelings about the scene. In this state, the negative feelings originally connected with the event will be diminished.

Negative Association-Positive Disassociation Pattern—The state by which an individual revivifies in the mind negative events and disassociates positive memories. This diminishes the good feeling associated with such positive events. For example, you may remember going to your senior prom and spilling a drink on yourself in an associative mode, so that you fully relive the negative experience. Whereas, when you think of dancing with your favorite person, you remember that in a disassociative mode, thus reducing the emotional aspects of the event.

VOCABULARY

Concomitant—Two or more events or conditions occurring at the same time.

Diagnostic Grid—A diagram that classifies information and past associations into categories for the purpose of diagnosis.

Disassociative State—Recreating a past experience from the perspective of an onlooker or observer. For example, you are viewing the event as a spectator and see yourself as a participant.

Dysfunction—Impaired or abnormal functioning.

Emotional Frames—The feelings associated with the recreation of a past event.

Informational Frames—The storage of the visual aspect of a past event.

Revivify or Revivification—Recreating the feelings and body sensations of a past experience.

Sorting—The manner in which a person categorizes information.

ASSOCIATED MEMORY MODE

To learn the roles that different memory modes play in affecting behavior, begin by looking at the picture in Illustration 5. After reviewing the picture, return to this page and read the explanation.

In Illustration 5, the woman is remembering a scene in a restaurant. In re-creating the image, she sees her hand around the glass of iced tea, and looking through her own eyes, she sees a waiter serving a tray in front of her on the other side of the table. If this memory is followed further, the woman sees the glass lifting upward toward her face and the tea emptying from the glass as she drinks the tea. This type of associative experience produces a very distinct positive emotional experience. This experience is called revivification and is classified as an associative mode.

In revivification, the individual relives the feelings and body sensations as felt during the actual experience. For example, remember the last time that a special person kissed you. If you remember this situation in an associative manner, you will step

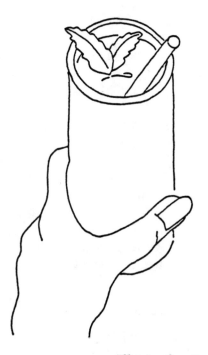

Illustration 5

inside your own body and see the other person's face coming toward you. You may even feel the person's arms around you. Hollywood directors have used this technique for years to emotionally influence and involve the audience in a story. Think of watching Clark Gable in *Gone with the Wind*. How many women felt Clark Gable's arms around them, and how many men felt the tears of Scarlet run down their own cheeks?

This phenomenon of revivification characterizes many successful films because it allows the viewer to participate. The human brain performs this same activity. When it does, it is classified as associative memory mode.

DISASSOCIATED MEMORY MODE

Before reading this section, look at Illustration 6, then return to the text.

The second major way of reviewing a memory is from a disassociative point of view. In Illustration 6, the same woman mentioned in the previous experience (Illustration 5) now sees herself from the perspective of an observer. In this memory, she sees her entire body sitting at a table, right elbow on the table, right hand on the chin, head slightly tilted up, hat on the head, left hand on the glass, and the waiter with a tray of salad. The difference is that she sees the scene from the perspective of an outside observer. She sees her entire body. It is as though she is watching a filmstrip of the experience. This is the disassociative memory mode.

This disassociative perspective may be experienced by rerunning a memory of yourself in the process of playing an athletic sport, such as tennis or bowling. In doing this, place the event on a movie or television screen, so that you can watch your actions and the actions of others completely. You will notice that you do not experience the emotions as if you were actually doing the event.

Remember the movie *Jaws*? Remember your feelings when the camera first took the perspective of being in the eyes of the victim? As you watched, you saw the shark with open mouth swimming directly at you. In that revivification, you were using

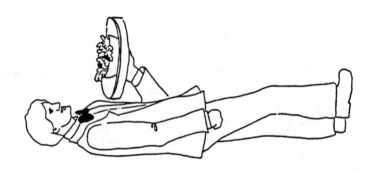

Illustration 6

the associative process. That associative process caused millions of people to avoid swimming in the ocean for many years after the film was shown. Contrast that with the lack of, or reduced intensity of, emotions that you felt as the camera moved away, so that you could see both the shark and person (disassociative process).

The use of these two techniques, association and disassociation, permitted the director of *Jaws* to build emotional peaks and valleys. The emotional peaks were times of association, whereas the emotional valleys were times of disassociation.

To experiment with these two brain processes or memory modes, watch a movie and notice the way the film maker utilizes the patterns of association and disassociation in order to build emotional peaks and valleys in the viewer.

Try this experiment. Think about cutting a ripe lemon in half. See your hands in front of you, cutting the thick, rough skin. As you see this, you may notice that you begin to salivate unconsciously. This is an example of the mind's associative ability.

DIAGNOSTIC MAP OF REPRESENTATIONAL SORTS

Using the associative and disassociative mental processes as a diagnostic model will help you better understand how your students' emotional responses can affect their learning states. Emotional responses and feelings can serve the function of increasing or impeding student learning. The mind processes and remembers experiences in either an associative or disassociative manner. It also sorts for sameness. Positive and negative memories can be sorted into the following grid, which reflects the Diagnostic Map of Representational Sorts:

Positive Associative	Positive Disassociative
Negative Associative	Negative Associative

In order to increase your understanding of how to use the diagnostic grid, several common diagnostic patterns will be described. These patterns will explain some of life's more recurring problems.

NEGATIVE ASSOCIATIVE AND POSITIVE DISASSOCIATIVE PATTERN

In a great many areas, such as inner city schools, one of the major problems that teachers face is stress overload. In some schools, stress is so great that many teachers' unions request or suggest combat pay. Burnout is becoming an increasingly common word within the teaching profession. Utilizing the grid as illustrated earlier in this chapter, imagine that you are a teacher in an inner city school and that during the course of the day, several unpleasant things have occurred. Being a dedicated and caring teacher, you review the events of the day after arriving home. If you are like many of the teachers and other professionals that the authors have encountered, you may find that you have reviewed the unpleasant events in an associative manner. This can be presented on the grid in the following manner:

Positive Associative	Positive Disassociative
Negative Associative	Negative Associative

Thus, you relive in your mind the associated negative event and disassociate the positive events. You then begin to reexperience the unpleasantness and stress of each of those events— negative feelings. Doing this repeatedly over a period of time reinforces the stress of the original event. You do not need to reexperience the events to restimulate feelings. Reliving it in your mind will not only bring back the feeling but, over a period of time, will intensify the feelings.

Many studies have shown that continued exposure to stress increases vulnerability to heart disease, blood pressure elevation, digestive problems, and a general decline in health status. When you review the events of a day, and you disassociate positive experiences and associate negative experiences, counterproductivity is generated.

DISASSOCIATING NEGATIVE FEELINGS

The following experiment will give you the opportunity to test the emotional impact that these learning patterns have on you and your students who have learned this particular sorting style. Remember one special day in your life, and then review your memories for that day. Notice whether the positive memories of that day are associated or disassociated, and whether the negative memories are associated or disassociated. You may begin to notice a familiar and unpleasant feeling begin to merge if you associated and revivified the negative instead of the positive associations. The authors have found that this is a relatively easy pattern to change.

If you find that you operate in this pattern, and you would like to disassociate this pattern, you can do this in the following way: a) Place the negative memories on a screen in front of you; b) Disassociate yourself by removing yourself from the scene and become an observer; c) Watch the memory of the scene run on the screen as if you were looking through a TV camera; d) You may also make the screen smaller and continue to move the screen further and further away from you. This will cause you to have the memory, but disassociate the negative feelings and experiences. This is depicted on the grid below.

Positive Associative	Positive Disassociative
Negative Associative	Negative Associative

This same approach is used to help students disassociate negative feelings. In clinical practice, the following questions are often raised: "If I disassociate my negative memories, so that I am no longer feeling bad, will this take away my ability to stop myself from doing negative actions?" "Will I become insensitive to the problems of others?"

The authors have found that learning does not depend upon having negative feelings as a method of changing or eliminating behavior. Instead, learning is directly related to the coding of information. For example, suppose you have a memory of raising your voice at a superior and that superior severely reprimands you. By reviewing this memory in a disassociative manner, the information needed to repeat the act will be stored in the scene that you see on the screen. The emotional impact will not be experienced. The sequence for this type of learning is that raising one's voice leads to reprimand. This data is contained in the information frames, rather than the emotional frames of reference.

Another example of this process is one that many individuals have experienced. Everyone, at some point in life, has touched a hot object. Instead of associating the experience and reliving the pain time and time again, it is remembered in a disassociated way. Learning results from the experience, without reliving the pain and the negative memory associated with the experience. In the future, objects which are hot will not be touched. The learning has been generalized.

REPROGRAMMING NEGATIVE ASSOCIATIONS WITH POSITIVE ASSOCIATIONS

The question of insensitivity can also be dealt with from the perspective of choices. To illustrate this important point, consider a student who has been reprimanded severely by an arithmetic teacher for numerous careless errors. Suppose the student associates this experience negatively with the teacher and arithmetic. Over a period of many days, the experience is relived many times, with the student reexperiencing the negative emotions each time. This can be depicted on the disassociative grid in the following manner:

Positive Associative	Positive Disassociative
Negative Associative	Negative Associative

To break this pattern, have the student sit in a chair and instruct the student to picture on a screen a recreation of the event as it actually happened. Have the student review the incident forward, then backward, on the screen. This will result in disassociating the experience.

After doing this procedure, have the student remember a *newly created pleasant experience*. Instruct the student to step inside the body and view this pleasant experience from the inside looking out. Instruct the student as follows: "See what you see, hear what hear, and feel what you feel." When the student is experiencing the pleasant emotion associated with the experience, anchor that experience so that the student can utilize that newly created positive experience and stage anytime it is needed or desired. This can create a positive internal state for learning. This process can be depicted on the grid as follows:

Positive Associative	Positive Disassociative
Negative Associative	Negative Associative

BREAKING NEGATIVE ASSOCIATION AND REPROGRAMMING POSITIVE ASSOCIATIONS FOR IMPROVED LEARNING

To illustrate this concept further, consider a student who tells the teacher that school and everything about school is hated by the student. The student's behavior pattern sorts for all the negative associations or unpleasant experiences the student has had previously. Attitudes toward school, school work, and homework are extremely negative. In order to help this student, the sorting pattern of associative negatives in school must be changed. In this case, the student has disassociated positives and associated negatives. (See the following grid.)

BEFORE

Positive Associative	Positive Disassociative
Negative Associative	Negative Associative

To break this sorting pattern or cycle, the student must be taught to disassociate negative experiences, and associate positive experiences in school. In other words, the pattern must be reversed. The student must learn to revivify positive associative experiences and disassociate negative disassociative experiences. This can be done by anchoring in the positive experiences and disassociating the negative experiences, as previously described. The changed pattern is depicted in the grid below:

AFTER

Positive Associative	Positive Disassociative
Negative Associative	Negative Associative

Consider this example: A student is observed to be fearful and shy. The student's shyness began in the second grade when he was scolded by a teacher for giggling during a spelling lesson. The student associated this experience and began to sort for experiences where teachers scolded him. By the end of third grade, he had collected and associated a negative set of memories. Because of the impact of the negatively associated memories, the student also disassociated positive experiences. The student became more and more withdrawn and became fearful of speaking or laughing in class which, in turn, began to affect his social relationships with his peers. A vicious cycle developed that started in the classroom and spread to the playground.

One of the authors did a change history (explained in Chapter 4) with the student. Together, they found the original associated negative scene. The author then taught the student to disassociate each of the negative experiences and to associate all of the positive resources and experiences in the school setting. Within two weeks, this shy and fearful student became accepted within the social setting by his peers and began to make contributions in the classroom setting. This process was aided by the teacher who reinforced each of the newly associated positive learnings.

As a further example of this concept, one of the authors had the opportunity of working with a large group in a workshop on choral singing. It quickly became apparent that many individuals were only mouthing the words to the music, while many others did not even attempt to participate. When we asked the participants who did not sing to remember earlier experiences of singing in groups, we found that many participants had been told, in either church or school-related choral events, to mouth the words and not sing. With very few exceptions, this precipitated a chain of associated negative memories about singing that lasted well into adulthood. It was interesting that when they disassociated these negative chain of events, a significant number of the persons reported real enjoyment of music. In the subjective experience of the authors, many were also able to demonstrate an average to high degree of musical talent.

From the above examples, you now have the skills necessary to diagnose and break negative sorting patterns and install positive patterns of behavior. As you utilize this diagnostic grid, and the skills presented in this chapter, you will find that both you and your students are more productive and happy.

Chapter 4
Collapsing Anchors or Unassociating Negative Associations

ADVANCED ORGANIZER

OVERVIEW

In this chapter, you will expand your knowledge of anchoring. You will discover how to collapse anchors by establishing two incompatible states and triggering them simultaneously. By utilizing such a procedure, you will have the ability to eliminate the detrimental effects of certain anchors (conditioned responses) on the learning process. In addition, you will appreciate the unconscious effect that anchoring exerts on all learning situations.

With this knowledge, you will be able to be more sensitive to "everyday occurrences" and their positive or negative influences on learning. Finally, you will be introduced to the technique of change history. This procedure will allow you to assist students in overcoming past negative conditionings that impede or interfere with learning.

CONCEPTS

Collapsing Anchors—The procedure by which two anchors for two incompatible responses are triggered at the same time. The more powerful (stronger) of the two anchors will dominate, resulting in the extinction of the weaker anchor. For example: An anchor for a strong, positive state is set kinesthetically on the person's right shoulder. An anchor for a negative state is set kinesthetically on the person's left shoulder. It is important that the positive anchor be the stronger of the two anchors. Both spots are then pressed simultaneously. This will result in the collapsing of the negative associations and the elimination of the negative feelings.

Change History—A procedure by which an individual is guided, by means of selective anchoring, to reexperience past situations. Resource states are then developed and installed in the subject's repertoire for current and future utilization. For example: By setting an anchor for test anxiety and going back through a student's past history, the anchor will serve to reestablish past scenes that were associated with feelings of anxiety. When the earliest experience is remembered, the student can be given new resources not previously known. Although the event has not been changed, the individual's perception has altered. The new perception can alter past negative feelings or states.

Resource State—A positive feeling that has been anchored or conditioned. This state can be elicited by the teacher or student touching a spot or by the use of some signal. This is a valuable technique for teachers to use because it permits an individual to overcome an undesirable state that interferes with learning.

VOCABULARY
Incompatible—Applies to two or more responses which cannot coexist due to specific characteristics or time factors.

Negative State—A condition which reflects past unpleasant experiences.

Perception—Interpretation of the elements of the environment through physical sensations.

COLLAPSING ANCHORS OR UNASSOCIATING NEGATIVE ASSOCIATIONS

Now that you have a way of identifying specific negative learning associations, what do you do with them? The technique of collapsing anchors involves triggering two anchors simultaneously, so that a more powerful positive anchor will short circuit or collapse the negative anchor. This idea is supported by the fact that, in neurology, two events cannot occupy the same physical space. The collapsing technique will demonstrate this fact and enhance your teaching effectiveness in the process.

Consider the example in which a student panics whenever the teacher says "test". The student's performance is severely impeded by past unpleasant associations or anchors with tests. To neutralize the negative associations or anchors, the teacher will need to find an anchor or association that is **more powerful and incompatible with** the negative anchor.

Taking the student aside (away from other students), the teacher should establish a kinesthetic anchor for the negative reaction to the word "test" (auditory) and for visual or kinesthetic stimuli accompanying the adverse reaction. The teacher then helps the student to identify a quiet, productive state that the student would like to experience in place of the negative state. Next, the teacher anchors that quiet, productive state on a different spot on the student's body. This anchor is tested, just as the negative anchor was tested to insure the return of the original state. The teacher then presses both spots simultaneously, holding them for ten seconds. The teacher releases the spot for the negative anchor, while maintaining the pressure on the spot for the positive anchor. This positive spot is held for five more seconds. After releasing the second spot, the teacher then tests the student to see if the original negative experience that occurred with the word "test" can be recaptured. This is done by pressing the original negative spot.

In most cases, students report that they no longer have the original negative reaction. If a student should report still having some reaction to the word "test," the teacher needs to stack additional positive anchors and repeat the process.

The experiences associated with past auditory anchors may be evoked by many words that have past associations with strong, emotional responses, including racial, ethnic, and religious slurs. One way to diffuse the effects of these negative associations is to use the collapsing anchors technique. It is only necessary to find an experience that is incompatible with and more powerful than the negative anchor and its response. After anchoring and testing both the negative anchor and the positive anchor, the two anchors are triggered simultaneously, resulting in the collapsing of the negative anchor. This nullifies the original negative emotional response. The negative anchor is then released while the positive anchor is held for five more seconds. The following steps are to be used when collapsing anchors.

STEP 1

The teacher and student mutually identify a situation that occurs repeatedly and interferes with learning.

STEP 2

Tell the student to remember the last time a specific negative feeling interfered with the student's learning. As the student remembers the specific situation, give the instructions, "See what you see, hear what you hear, and feel what you feel." (Be sure that the student is associated with the experienced state.) When the internal negative feeling is experienced, touch the student on a specific place on the body (arm, hand, or shoulder) and hold that spot for ten seconds. Release the touch. Wait just a few seconds, then touch the same spot to see if it brings back the same state. If it does not bring back the same state, repeat the first two steps. If it does, proceed to the next step.

STEP 3

Ask the student to select a specific positive feeling. Instruct the student to go back to the last time that particular positive state was experienced. Ask the student to, "See what you see, hear what you hear, and feel what you feel." Tell the student to slightly move a finger when that state is being experienced. When the student signals with a finger, anchor that state. Press a spot on the student's body and hold it for ten seconds, then release that spot or anchor. Touch that same spot within a few minutes to test the anchor.

STEP 4

Touch both anchors at the same time. It is imperative that you press **the same spot with the same pressure.** Hold both spots **simultaneously** for **ten seconds.** Then release the first (negative) anchor. Wait five seconds, then slowly release the second (positive) anchor.

STEP 5

Ask the student to go back to the original negative feeling state and to pay attention to **"What is different?"** If the student can no longer experience the negative feelings, you have collapsed the anchors. If the student is still able to experience part of the negative feeling state, you will need to anchor another positive feeling state in the same location as the first positive anchor, and repeat the above steps. This latter procedure is called "stacking anchors."

When utilizing the technique of collapsing anchors, the two states selected must have comparable value or meaning to the student. It would not be advisable to have a state of licking your favorite ice cream flavor as the positive state and losing a job as the negative state. Furthermore, they should be in the same experiential reference, e.g., relaxation versus anxiety, fear versus confidence, etc.

One of the authors recalled a situation that demonstrated the power of anchoring in a university setting. The university at which he was teaching used an exam book for all testing. The exam book was blue, carried the university seal on the cover, and was quite attractive. However, the students' perceptions of these books were not positive. The teacher inadvertently carried some exam books into a class where an exam was not scheduled. The effect on the students was remarkable. Many students protested and complained of unfair treatment. Other students reported that they actually felt physically ill, and one student even left the room and had to be called back to class. An attractive blue book had become a powerful negative anchor.

Situations similar to the above are found in many classrooms and at all levels of education. Sometimes, it is the exam book; other times, it is the visual anchor of a stack of ditto sheets. It may even be the olfactory anchor of the smell of ditto fluid or the auditory anchor of the teacher saying, "Take everything off your desk." In any case, the results are similar. Students report increased heart rates, stomach distress, cold hands, and other manifestations of anxiety. When faced with such a situation, the teacher is advised to consider using the technique of collapsing anchors.

For example, assume that the negative anchor for anxiety was the sight of the blue exam book. The teacher should present the blue book to the student with the instruction to recreate the feelings attached to this stimulus. When the feelings are at the highest point, the student is instructed to squeeze the left hand into a tight fist. After setting this additional negative anchor, it should be tested to see if it brings back the negative state. Next, the teacher asks the student to imagine a time when calmness and confidence were experienced. When the feeling of this state are at the highest point, the student is told to squeeze the right hand into a tight fist. After this anchor is tested and verified, the student is instructed to squeeze both fists at the same time. The resulting state will serve to reduce the effect of the negative anchor. With many individuals, it may be necessary to stack many positive anchors to overcome the cumulative effect of years of anxiety controlled by the negative anchor. Once a strong positive state has been achieved, it can also serve as a "magic button" or resource state for future times of stress.

The authors have found that the process of collapsing anchors with "magic buttons" works extremely well in changing negative behavior and negative learning states with most students. Occasionally, associative and disassociative techniques may need to be used together. The need may arise when the original stimulus is so severe that it is difficult to find a positive anchor or anchors strong enough to overcome the negative associations. In the course of a lifetime, even in the relatively short life span of a young student, the anchoring process sometimes has associated negative internal states which are so severe that they are essentially repressed. Traditionally, attempts at changing past personal experiences have been designed to either have the person "work it through" or ignore it. The fact is that we cannot change an individual's past, but we can change an individual's perceptions of the past.

For example, think back to a time when you were extremely embarrassed. Even now, as you think about it, you feel embarrassed. Now think about another time when you were extremely embarrassed, yet you can look back and laugh about the situation or experience. In both instances, a situation occurred which stimulated the embarrassment. Notice that in neither case did you alter the facts, yet your perceptions were different.

In the first instance, your perception remains fixed and frozen as it was at that time, while in the second instance, your perception has changed. A technique is needed that will allow the perceptions about past events to be altered in a quick and efficient manner. Anchoring can bring about such a change. However, the technique of change history is an even more sophisticated concept of anchoring and can be applied to more difficult or complicated situations.

CHANGE HISTORY

To illustrate this concept, consider the teacher who became timid and shy any time the principal entered the room. In working with this teacher, one of the authors anchored shyness and timidity for a specific incident when the principal had entered the classroom. Working alone with the teacher after school, this state of shyness and timidity was anchored.

The next task was to determine how this anchor of shyness and timidity was associated with the negative state. The teacher was requested to pretend that he was riding a light beam back through time to the situation in which he first developed these feelings. The anchor was pressed and held constant as the teacher went back in time on the light beam (the negative anchor) to the earliest point in time when that state could be identified. Since the brain sorts for sameness, this anchor became a sorting mechanism for experiences containing this negative emotional state.

COLLAPSING ANCHORS

Most individuals are able to remember very quickly several different experiences, going back through time until they get to the original experience. In this case, the teacher's earliest memory of shyness and timidity was in childhood when the principal mildly disciplined him in school for an inappropriate behavior. It was easy to understand how shyness and timidity became a negative anchor and how that anchor was easily repeated and reinforced in the presence of authority figures from that earliest point to the present time. Because anchored states are repeated, they tend to build on each other, reinforcing the same negative response, thus creating a pattern that becomes automatic. This explains how the teacher learned a pattern that limited the responses that could be offered in a particular situation.

Continuing to work with the teacher, the next step was to identify a resource state for him in the original negative experience. The easiest way to identify this state was to ask the person "What did you need back then in the way of a resource, so that you could have a different perception and a different internal experience to the principal disciplining you?" Or, "What do you know now that you did not know then that would have made the situation easier?" The teacher identified that he needed to feel confident and to know that the experience would end. The task now was to find a context in which he was experiencing an unpleasant situation, but knew it would end.

The newly identified resource state was anchored on a different location than the original negative anchor. This anchor was placed where the teacher could trigger it conveniently. The teacher was then asked to relive the memory of the original situation of the principal disciplining him, but this time, the resource anchor was triggered and held. The process of triggering the resource state while reliving the original situation enabled the teacher to gain a different perspective and perception of the original event. (NOTE: Do not trigger the negative anchor when running the resource anchor, as this may cause the weaker one to collapse.)

The brain sorts for sameness, so the next step was to help the teacher activate his new resources the next time he encountered the principal (or other authority figures). This was done by asking him to look into the future to a time when he would encounter the principal. In imagining a specific situation with the principal, the teacher was instructed to trigger the new resource anchor. The teacher will no longer experience shyness and timidity and will be able to relate positively and productively to the principal.

In some cases, it may be necessary to increase the power of the resource state by stacking anchors. In stacking anchors, the same spot is used with the same pressure, while a new resource state is relived, thus anchoring the second resource. There are times when stacking a third anchor may be desirable in order to maximize effectiveness of the resource state.

To illustrate this concept in the classroom with a student, consider a fourth grade student who was shy and withdrawn whenever she was called upon to speak in class. Although her written work demonstrated that she had the necessary knowledge to speak in front of the class, she stammered and said, "I don't know." The teacher privately asked the student to remember the last time she experienced feeling uncomfortable. The teacher then anchored that state. Holding the anchor, the student was told to go back in time and remember other times when she felt similar uncomfortable states. The student's earliest memory was in the second grade when she performed in a play. As she started to speak, one of the parents suddenly popped up and took her picture with a flash camera. The disruption caused her to forget her lines and resulted in a great deal of laughter and mocking from the other students. This event became associated/anchored with her internal state of being uncomfortable when speaking before groups.

In continuing to work with the student, the teacher then questioned what resources she needed in order to be able to be comfortable in the original situation. The student could not identify anything that would have helped her in the original situation. At this point, the teacher had to be creative in finding resources for the student. (Ask yourself how you would have handled the situation and what resources this student needed.) The experience, as it happened in the past, could not be changed.

However, the following question could be asked: What did the student need then? The student needed to be able to take a minute to organize her thoughts and to recover her internal image of the lines she was to speak. She needed to recognize that the students laughing at her was a passing event.

In further discussion, the teacher asked the student if she had ever forgotten something momentarily and then remembered it. The student described going to the store for her mother and momentarily forgetting what she was to purchase. Upon remembering what it was, she felt good. The teacher then anchored that state and asked the student if she could remember a time when a group of students laughed at her and she felt comfortable about it. She remembered that, in learning how to play basketball, a group of girls in her neighborhood had laughed and teased each other including her when they missed the basket. She felt comfortable with it because she knew they were only kidding. The teacher then anchored in this second state of feeling comfortable in the same spot as the first state of feeling comfortable, thus making a more powerful resource anchor by stacking.

While triggering the resource anchor and holding it, the teacher asked the student to go back to the original experience of performing in front of a group, with the flashbulb flashing and her forgetting her lines, then progress forward to the present experience of feeling uncomfortable in having to speak in front of a group. Pressing the resource anchor while having the student progress from the initial memory to the present changed the student's perception and feeling state from negative to positive. The next time the student was asked to speak in front of a group, she did so with confidence, feeling comfortable and remembering her lines.

The technique of change history has innumerable applications both within and outside of educational settings. Your imagination will open up unlimited applications.

Chapter 5
Understanding And Utilizing Disassociative States of Learning

ADVANCED ORGANIZER

OVERVIEW

In this chapter, you will learn the powerful effect of disassociation on the learning process. You will recognize situations where this phenomenon has occurred in your life experiences and, perhaps more importantly, when it could have reduced your anxiety. By learning how to use disassociation with yourself and with others, you will have gained a powerful educational tool. With this new skill, you will have the ability to remove learning blocks or phobic responses, thereby enriching the life experiences of your students.

CONCEPTS

Disassociative State—An internal state by which an individual relives a situation from the viewpoint of an observer. In this state, you recreate the memory, and you see yourself as a participant acting out the drama. In so doing, you disassociate yourself from the activities. In such a state, painful feelings and emotions are reduced. This a powerful tool for removing past learning blocks in students. If past emotional responses to traumatic events can be eliminated, new learnings can be allowed to emerge.

Disassociative State of Learning—A state in which being disassociated from a situation serves to improve learning and/or performance. For example, a student who is not emotionally upset by reliving past failures will perform better than one who is hampered by past failures. Teachers will find this technique useful for helping students overcome negative influences of past events.

Here and Now Anchor—An established anchor that is utilized when guiding a person back through previous traumatic events. It serves as a reality check. It is used to reduce the possibility of over-responding to past events. For example, holding a student's hand when recreating an unpleasant experience, acts as a reminder of the present. A slight squeeze would serve to bring the student back to reality if the situation proved to be too traumatic.

Phobic Response—The association of a specific sensory stimulus with a past traumatic event. Future presentations of the stimulus results in the recreation of the unpleasant responses. For example, a student was frightened when his mother became separated from him while they were on an elevator in a crowded department store. The subsequent panic became attached to the stimulus of an elevator. Conceivably, the student could become an adult and continue to display the fear response whenever an elevator ride is required. In extreme cases, the individual may avoid elevators at all times.

VOCABULARY

Freeze Frame—Stopping the running of a movie (real or imaginary) at a particular point and concentrating on one frame or picture.

Metaphor—A comparison which uses one object or event as the equivalent of another object or event.

Phobic Response—A persistent and unreasonable fear.

Psychosomatic Illness—Physical disorders caused by mental or emotional disturbances.

UNDERSTANDING AND UTILIZING
DISASSOCIATIVE STATES OF LEARNING

With an awareness of the power of association, the number of times that teachers and students may need to disassociate in order to be at peak efficiency is amazing! Few teachers have taught without experiencing a classroom emergency, e.g., a student has fallen and was severely cut or knocked unconscious. The teacher who dealt with the emergency in an associative manner became flooded with emotion and often became paralyzed or ineffective as a result of that emotion. However, the teacher who disassociated and remained calm is undoubtedly more effective in such situations.

Think of the times when a teacher has been called into another classroom to assist a colleague because the colleague was not able to cope with the emergency.

Described in terms of the diagnostic grid model, the colleague became paralyzed in an associative state during the emergency and thus became overwhelmed.

In fact, many people have experienced some type of major or minor trauma e.g., car accident, death of a loved one, being involved in a fight, etc. If these persons tend to revivify the experience again and again, they also suffer much or all of the stress of the original experience in an associated manner. This is an important concept in the identifying and referring of students who have been abandoned, abused, and/or sexually molested. This national problem, involving hundreds of thousands of children, continues to escalate. Because of the teacher's involvement with students on a daily basis, the teacher becomes a "front line" person. Thus, it is important that the teacher at least be able to better understand and help students having emotional reactions in associative states.

In this chapter, an explanation will be given on how to create disassociative states for specific learning situations. Disassociation will be described from an educational standpoint rather than from a therapeutic standpoint. **Therapeutic interventions are best deferred to appropriate psychotherapeutic professionals. In using disassociation, the areas of abuse, sexual molestation,**

and other serious traumas should be avoided in working with students in the school setting, and appropriate referrals should be made! The teacher must be concerned primarily with disassociation in terms of blocks to learning in educational settings, e.g., speaking before a classroom, fear of failure, fear of being ridiculed, fear of rejection, etc.

Consider the following case in which one of the authors was consulted. A ten year old student was an A-B student with an I.Q. of 120+. He was described as bright, friendly, and having a good sense of humor. However, the student panicked every time the teacher gave any criticism about his exams or essays. When the author met the student, he was exactly as described by the teacher. In order to further evaluate the student, the author produced one of the student's past tests. The student was asked how he could have missed such a simple problem. The student became anxious, nervous, and tearful. The author then asked the student if he would like to have a new behavior for such instances, rather than becoming so upset. The student responded, "Of course!" Most students find this type of emotional state embarrassing, but do not recognize it as an impediment to both present and future learning.

In this case, the student was asked to go back and remember the last time he had become anxious, nervous, and tearful. The student identified the incident just described. The student was asked to revivify that negative state, which the author then anchored and tested. After establishing the negative anchor, the author asked the student to take his hand and squeeze it lightly and to know that he was "Here and Now" in this room. The author thus established both a negative anchor, which produced the negative state, and a "Here and Now" anchor. The author asked the student to stand up and join him behind the chair. The student was then instructed to observe himself sitting in the chair as though he were watching a television screen. (See Illustration 7.)

Instructions were given to the student to watch his life running backwards until he found his earliest memory of feeling anxious, nervous, and tearful, and to then freeze that frame on the screen. The author then stated, "Watch yourself in the chair

Screen:
Framework
with the
Younger Self

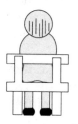

Visualization
of Student
in Chair

Teacher Standing
With Student
Behind Chair

Illustration 7

watching the movie of that experience."

A disassociation process was thus established. The student was instructed to watch the movie until he learned something he did not know before watching the movie. (An instruction such as this frequently helps the student to develop a different perception and to learn something not previously known.) The student was instructed to tell the younger self on the screen that he was from his world of tomorrow (or from the year _____) and would answer any questions that the younger self had about that earlier experience, as well as comfort the younger self as needed. The student was told to bring the new learning with him to the present time. Instructions then were given to turn off the television set and return to his body in the chair.

In another example, disassociation was used to overcome an undesirable school-related behavior. The fourteen year old student had become increasingly troublesome in school. She had developed numerous psychosomatic illnesses and was a truancy problem.

In doing the change history, the author asked the student to go back in time to a particular situation. The student became pale, her breathing changed—becoming rapid and shallow, and she began crying hysterically. All the pacing skills available to the author were used in order to get the student calmed down. The student described the situation she had been viewing and related this story: "My mother was driving me to school when a truck came around the corner, ran a stop sign, and hit our car. My mother and I spent nearly three weeks in the hospital. "

The incident had occurred at the age of ten, and her school truancy began at age eleven. After talking with the student, the author noticed a phobic pattern associated with leaving her house for school. The author switched to the disassociative pattern and established a "here and now" anchor. The student was then instructed to go behind the chair (with the author) and observe herself in the chair, watching her life on a television screen. She watched herself going back in life to the time of the accident. She was told to reassure the younger self (the self at the time of the accident that she was watching) that both she and her mother had survived. She was instructed to nurture and comfort the younger self. The student was brought back to the present with the instruction to identify and use this new learning. The author then told the student to turn off the television screen and return to her body on the chair.

In another case of school phobia, a fourteen year old student suddenly developed panic attacks when he prepared to leave for school in the morning. These attacks became so incapacitating that the student was placed on home bound instruction. The teacher used the disassociative technique as described previously to eliminate this phobic response.

Both cases illustrate how phobias may be developed. Both students had experienced a traumatic incident. Reviewing the scene in the earliest memory in an associated perspective was very traumatic and left both students feeling out of control and in a panic state. In both cases, there was a single learning that was recorded in visual memory. Its negative kinesthetic effects became associated and generalized with going to school (as described below):

In this simple formula, we notice that the student does not need to experience the original trauma. The student does experience the association that has been associated with the trauma. In these two cases, school stimulated the phobic response. In both incidents, the students reexperienced the phobic response as the memory was relived and played back in the associated mode.

To further describe this process, consider the following metaphor. When a student is watching the original negative associated experience, it is as if it were recorded on a videotape. This tape seems to be in a loop in the mind that plays over and over, so that the actual moment of trauma or phobic learning becomes frozen in time. If a trauma or phobic response exists, and it is remembered and visualized, it plays to a certain point, then restarts. Each time it starts, it revivifies the experience, so that the associated kinesthetic state is experienced again and again. It is as if the film in a person's head gets stuck and keeps repeating the same loop.

This is why the disassociative technique works so well. It allows the person to watch the complete scene from beginning to end and vice versa, and from an entirely new perspective. Thus, the traumatic material is allowed to have both a beginning and an end. It allows the individual to have closure and completion. It further separates the picture from the emotion. As you use these techniques, the possibilities for utilization will become more apparent. The following is an outline of the disassociative technique:

1. Establish and maintain rapport.
2. Establish an anchor for the "Here and Now" state. If the student gets stuck in an associative place with the original event, the "Here and Now" anchor may be used to return the student to the present.
3. Ask the student to remember the last time the reaction occurred. (Often, the technique of change history may be needed to get to the original event.)
4. Anchor that state, interrupt the state, then test the anchor.
5. Instruct the student to place that scene on an imaginary television or movie screen with all the attendant feelings.
6. Tell the student to run the movie to the most traumatic part and freeze that frame. Tell the student to imagine floating out of his/her body and watch from behind the chair or a position behind.
7. Anchor this disassociative state.
8. Tell the student to rerun the scene until s/he learns something new or something not previously remembered from this perspective. When the student acknowledges this, continue to Step 9.
9. Tell the student to talk to the younger self on the screen, stating "I am from your tomorrow and this is what I have learned . . . ." The student is then told to nurture and comfort the younger self. The student is to accept the younger self as part of the present existence and to bring the new learning to

the present. (NOTE: A modification that proves to be most effective is to anchor in a calm and relaxed state prior to the disassociative state and to trigger that anchor as the student comforts the younger self.)

10. To further solidify the disassociated state, have the student run the movie scene backward, making the scene smaller and smaller. Fade the contrast until the scene becomes a small dot, then have the small dot spin out into space.

11. Remember to check and future pace your work.

When removing a phobia, caution should be observed to be sure the fear did not serve a protective function. If the fear does serve as a protective function, appropriate new learning strategies have to be installed.

For example, one of the authors worked with a school phobic who was taken to and from school each day by a parent. The student lived on a dead end street with little traffic. After the student was cured of the phobia and walked to school with classmates, it was important that the student be given information about traffic, speed of cars, and general traffic safety. The student previously had not had to consider such information.

In conclusion, this technology is so powerful that it is suggested that additional training be obtained in the use of these methods. These methods can be most effective when used skillfully and appropriately.

In addition, **it is important to remember that as a teacher, your concern is with educational problems rather than with deep-seated emotional problems. Refer serious problems to the proper professionals!**

Chapter 6
Learning Styles And Learning Patterns

ADVANCED ORGANIZER

OVERVIEW

In this chapter, you will learn how to identify a student's preferred learning style. You will be cautioned that a student's preferred learning style may not be the most proficient or efficient way of learning. You, the teacher, will share in some of the more recent research and methodologies that have proven to hold promise for developing optimum learning. In this sharing, you will learn how to extract and code individual student learning patterns. These learning patterns will enable you to teach your student more efficient ways of learning.

CONCEPTS

Effective Communication for Effective Learning—This concept reflects the NLP philosophy that teachers are responsible for insuring that each student's communication matches the preferred or most efficient learning style of the student. Unless communication channels are congruent between teachers and students, learning will not be optimum. For example, if a student's primary representational system is visual, it is the responsibility of the teacher to insure that the mode of communication reflects that channel. In such a case, a teacher would do well to utilize visual predicates, as well as instructional techniques that involve visual materials.

Eye Accessing Cue—The directional movement of the eye.

Learning Patterns—The selection and sequence of representational systems utilized by a student in problem-solving or task situations. For example, when presented with a verbal math problem, the student may repeat the question aloud, make a visual picture of the problem, and give an auditory answer. This pattern would be "auditory—visual—auditory" (coded A, V, A). The pattern would be determined by the teacher observing eye accessing cues and predicate usage.

VOCABULARY

Comparative Analysis—A comparison of two or more patterns or strategies to discover the most effective pattern.

Right Hemisphere—The hemisphere of the brain that deals with visual material.

Left Hemisphere—The hemisphere of the brain that deals with auditory material.

Neurological Face Map—An illustration designed to reference eye movements and the corresponding representational system for the majority of the population. (See Appendix 3.)

LEARNING STYLES AND LEARNING PATTERNS

There is an increasing awareness among educators everywhere that some of the traditional methods of teaching are not conducive to the optimal learning of students. For example, placing high pressure on students to motivate high achievement frequently has the opposite effect. This pressure usually produces undue anxiety and frustration. Even worse, it destroys both the creativity and the enjoyment of learning. It can ultimately repress the innate potential of students.

Many studies have been done on how to teach others effectively and efficiently. As many educators expound one method, an equal number of educators will disagree with that same method. Some theories have been tested in the academic community, while others have not (or have yet to be evaluated). The works of Dilts, Bandler, Grinder, and others have contributed greatly to the progress made in this area.

LEVEL I: EFFECTIVE COMMUNICATION FOR EFFECTIVE LEARNING

In relating to others (in whatever capacity), there is nothing more important than communication. Communication is the means by which knowledge is imparted, needs are made known, and by which thoughts and feelings are conveyed. Webster (1983) defines communication as "an act or instance of transmitting: 1. Information communicated; 2. A verbal or written message; 3. An exchange of information; 4. A system for communication; 5. Personnel engaged in communication, a process by which meanings are exchanged between individuals through a common system of symbols; 6. The technology of the transmission of information."

In these definitions, the theme of transmitting a message or the exchange of a message or information by individuals can easily be seen. The main purpose of our educational system is essentially to transmit messages and information to students. This then helps them to understand and adjust to a rapidly changing world, as well as to impact on that world in a beneficial way. This search continues for better ways to communicate with students.

One very effective model of communication focuses on how information is processed. This model may expand your beliefs and perceptions about the processing of information and help you to improve your teaching skills.

In this model, the teacher begins by watching the student's eyes. All of the nerves of the body are connected in some way to the nerves in back of the eyes. External stimuli is transmitted from the eyes to different parts of the brain. Different areas of the brain are thus stimulated by the movement of the eyes. The location or direction of a student's eye movement can convey which area of the brain being stimulated is significant in receiving information, interpreting and the storing of information. (Dilts, 1976). Information can be transmitted by the teacher in such a way that it is interpreted easily and reliably by the learner. To do so, the teacher must be cognizant of eye movements and brain function in relationship to learning.

In training practitioners of NLP, the authors have observed confusion with the words left and right when identifying eye movements because the relevance of left and right reverses from the observer to the observed. Therefore, it is useful to apply the following framework: Redraw the illustration labeled Neurological Face Map (see Appendix 4) on a large sheet of paper. After you have done this, cut out the eyes. Superimpose it in front of the student's face with whom you are working. Notice the left and right markings on the picture. These markings are in relation to the **observer.** (In the text, we will indicate whether the reference point is from the student or the observer.)

The first step is for the teacher to become aware of what eye movements mean in terms of processing sensory information. Remember the concept of calibrating external states to internal states. Similarly, the student's first eye movement must be calibrated according to where it goes in response to specific sensory questions or stimuli. (Use the questions in Appendix 5 as a guide for calibrating.) The neurological organization of most right-handed people will be discussed. It is important to remember that individual calibration is always necessary.

When a student accesses certain portions of the brain, a specific class of words accompany that process. Observe a student who is asked to recall a visual experience, such as "What does the bathroom in your house or apartment look like?" Usually, the student's eyes will go up and to the observer's right. This means that the student received the information and accessed the visual part (right hemisphere) of the brain to recall information about the bathroom. If the same student were asked, "What would you look like with long, purple hair?" the student's first eye movement should be up and to the observer's left. The right hemisphere of the brain is again accessed, but this time, it creates a visual image in an attempt to see what one would look like with long, purple hair. When the eyes go up and to the observer's left, visual images are being constructed or created.

Visual images are stored or created in the right hemisphere of the brain.

Consider a statement that involves auditory content, such as, "Remember the sound of your mother speaking to you at an early age." Notice the eyes of the observed student going toward the student's left ear. The student is accessing the auditory hemisphere of the brain (Dilts, 1978). When the eyes are level and move toward the student's left ear (observer's right), this indicates to the observer that the student is engaging in the auditory recall of words or sounds. When a student tries to pronounce a new word or name, notice that the eyes move level and across to the student's right ear. This indicates that the student is engaged in the auditory construction of sounds or words. Whenever a student is talking to him/herself, you will notice that the student's eyes are looking down and toward the student's left.

Suppose the student is asked a question concerning a feeling about something. For example, "How does it feel to step from a warm, heated room into the cold outside?" Notice that the student's eyes go down and to the observer's left. The student is accessing the kinesthetic portion of the brain.

In this text, emotion is a kinesthetic response that can be broken down into external or internal sensory experiences. For example, think of the last time you were angry. Allow yourself to re-experience that feeling of anger. Notice specific experiences in your breathing, stomach, jaw, arms, etc. These sensations correspond to your eyes being down and to your right.

When a student's eyes look straight ahead, as if staring into space, the visual part of the brain is engaged. The student is making internal pictures. Educators traditionally have thought that such actions of a student meant the student was dreaming or not paying attention. This may, or may not, be the case. In fact, it may mean that the student is processing the data visually in order to make sense of it.

Try an experiment. Give a student a math problem and ask the student to do it without use of paper. When the student seems to look ahead and stare into space, wave your hand in front of the student. The internal images will be interrupted, consequently causing confusion. At this point, ask the student to state the problem and give the answer to the problem. Most people are unable to comply with this request.

The initial or first movement of the student's eye in response to a situation or communication will henceforth be referred to as the student's lead system. The lead system is a sensory processing of the eyes which engage the brain in seeking some form of information. It is one of the first steps in mapping a person's pattern for processing information. (Note: Eye accessing does not always occur unless the individual is searching for information.)

As the teacher communicates with a student, it is important to observe and determine the lead system most often used by the student to process information. The teacher can then communicate with the student in the identified lead system (visual, auditory, or kinesthetic), thus effecting more productive communication and learning.

For example, if the student's eyes predominantly move up to the right or left, it is calibrated that the student communicates best visually. The teacher should communicate verbally to this student in visual language, such as **see, view, perceive, watch, perspective,** etc. By doing this, the teacher matches the way the student initially processes information. If the teacher uses visual language, and the student's lead system is kinesthetic, the teacher is mismatching the student's communication processing.

The learning process is enhanced tremendously when the teacher is flexible and communicates the knowledge, concept, or skill in the same mode as the student. For example, a student says, "I can't **grasp** what you are saying" (eyes down and to the observer's left) and the teacher replies, "Can't you **see** how the water flows?" The teacher is using visual language for communication and the student is accessing kinesthetically. Ideally, the teacher should say to a kinesthetic student, "**Feel** the way the water flows through this junction," rather than "**See** how the water flows through this junction."

Study the Neurological Face Map in Appendix 3. This is the first level of mapping a student's learning style. Be aware that this level only provides the fundamental beginnings of mapping learning styles and patterns. Remember that the Neurological Face Map given in Appendix 3 is only representative of the way **most** right-handed people are neurologically organized. A student's lead system may be verified by calibrating the student's eye movements with the internal sensory states. To do this, use the calibration questions in Appendix 5. In progressing through the other levels, your skills and proficiency at identifying and understanding learning styles and learning patterns will be further developed.

LEVEL II: LEARNING PATTERNS

Analyzing a student' learning pattern is a sophisticated process which begins with and builds on the identification and matching of a student's lead system. While talking and listening to a student, observe the first three predicates used by the student. Predicates are verbs, adverbs, and adjectives that a student uses to describe personal experiences. If a student uses predicates that are visual in nature (see, view, perceive, etc.), a visual representational system is being used. If the student uses auditory predicates (hear, say, sounds like, etc.), an auditory representational system is being used. If the student uses kinesthetic predicates (feel, grasp, get a hold of, etc.), a kinesthetic representational system is being used. For example, the student says, "I understand math better when I **see** it done slowly by the teacher, **write** the facts several times, then **say** them to myself."

Using the Neurological Face Map, analyze the learning pattern of the student. In this instance, the student's eyes went up upon saying, ". . . when I **see** . . . , " and the predicate was visual. As the student said, "**write** the facts . . . ," the student's eyes moved downward and to the observer's left, and the predicate was kinesthetic. The student's eyes then moved downward and to the observer's right in saying, ". . . **say** them to myself," thus corresponding to auditory internal talk. See the diagram below for a description and sequencing of the aforementioned student's learning pattern:

$$V \quad — \quad K \quad — \quad A$$

Note that this pattern will not always occur consistently with this student. Therefore, look for patterns over a number of instances in order to establish and verify a student's dominant learning pattern. This is a further refinement of calibration.

The next step is to determine if this initial pattern is representative of what the student does in learning most memory tasks. It is particularly important that the teacher also determine whether the student's current learning pattern is effective and conducive to the student's optimal learning. Some students have learning patterns that are not effective for that particular subject. In such cases, the teacher should help the student to develop another more effective learning pattern. The preferred learning pattern is the simplest one that enables the student to reach the goal.

For example, a student is observed using the pattern V-K-A successfully when learning addition. The teacher observes that the student changes the learning pattern when learning multiplication. The following pattern might occur: The student is **verbally** presented the multiplication facts; the student verbally **repeats** the facts after the teacher, then **writes** them down. The learning pattern is described as A-A-K. The teacher also observes that the student is having difficulty remembering the multiplication facts.

In analyzing the situation, the teacher goes back to the point in math problems when the student was successful. The learning pattern for this successful phase of learning addition is compared with the learning pattern currently being used for learning multiplication. Note the difference between the two learning patterns: V-K-A versus A-A-K. In order to teach multiplication, duplicate the first pattern (V-K-A) which was used successfully in teaching addition. Thus, the teacher will instruct the student in multiplication facts by: a) writing them on the chalkboard, b) having the student **write** them, and c) having the student **say** them to him/herself. The learning pattern of V-K-A is thus duplicated, and the student will have less difficulty in learning multiplication.

It is important to note that in teaching, teachers also employ specific patterns to which students may respond with their own unique, dominant learning patterns or adjusted learning patterns. These patterns may, or may not, be effective for optimal learning. In the example given above, the teacher changed from a visual pattern to an auditory pattern. The student's pattern changed in response to the teacher's pattern.

In order to effectively teach multiplication to the student, the teacher should revert to the original pattern and duplicate it. The student then duplicates the original learning pattern of V-K-A. The teacher must now do a comparative analysis to determine how well the student is learning multiplication with the original pattern. All learning patterns must be tested by comparative analysis. Comparative analysis entails comparing one learning pattern with another learning pattern in order to note which pattern is more efficient in producing the desired outcome.

The important concept is this: The teacher must observe and listen to the student to find instances of how the student learns best. This learning pattern is extracted, applied to other learning situations, and compared analytically to determine the effectiveness for a particular student and a particular subject matter.

An effective learning pattern for one subject may, or may not, be effective for another subject. This is comparable to the successful teacher who becomes a principal. If the principal uses the same patterns in managing colleagues or teachers that were used with students in the past, much resistance may be encountered. Certain successful patterns used in managing students may be useful with colleagues. Patterns may also be extracted from other successful principals.

Similarly, a student may not have an effective learning pattern for a particular subject. The pattern used successfully in another subject also may not be successful in this particular subject. A learning pattern may then be extracted from a student who does well in that particular subject. This pattern should be taught to the student having difficulty with that subject.

LEVEL III: MORE ABOUT LEARNING PATTERNS

In extracting the students' learning patterns, the teacher must also determine internal and external features of the patterns. Internal means that the student went "inside," had an inner feeling, talked to him/herself, and/or made an internal picture.

Internal seeing is noted as Vi (visual, internal). Information and pictures that are remembered from the past and associated with the present are noted as Vr (visual, remembered). Internal talking is noted as Ai (auditory, internal). Internal feeling is noted as Ki (kinesthetic, internal). Similarly, for external factors: Seeing something externally is symbolized as Ve (visual, external). Hearing something from "outside" is symbolized as Ae (auditory, external). Physically touching and feeling are symbolized as Ke (kinesthetic, external).

To apply the Level III concept of identifying learning patterns, the teacher must listen to a student's predicates and note whether they are internal or external and which sensory modality is being used. The notation or recording process may be summarized, as follows:

Vi: Visual, remembered (internally remembered, generated from the past). Example: I can see a doll I had at the age of two.

Ai: Auditory, internal (internally generated auditory representation). Example: I can hear myself saying hello.

Ki: Kinesthetic, internal (internally generated kinesthetic representations). Example: I feel happy inside.

Ve: Visual, external (externally generated visual representations). Example: I see the sun in the picture on the wall.

Ae: Auditory, external (externally generated auditory representations). Example: I hear laughter in your voice.

Ke: Kinesthetic, external (externally generated kinesthetic representations). Example: Your touch is warm and gentle.

To further illustrate how this technique is used, the following examples are offered:

Example 1: A student learns effectively by looking at something, asking questions about it, then feeling an internal knowing. The learning pattern is coded as Ve-Ae-Ki. In order to teach photosynthesis to this student, the teacher should: 1) Present a picture of photo-synthesis in a plant (Ve); 2) Pose a rhetorical question about photosynthesis (Ae); and 3) Make a feeling statement about photosynthesis (Ke). The teacher might say, "As you **see** the picture of photosynthesis, you might be **asking** yourself several questions, such as: 'How does light get changed into energy?' As you ask questions, you may **feel** a growing curiosity." With these instructions, the teacher has matched the teaching pattern (Ve-Ae-Ki) with the student's learning pattern (Ve-Ae-Ki) to produce effective learning. (Note: Ae could be Ai if the student did not voice the question.)

NOTE: It is important to take several samples of the student's learning patterns. Observe which pattern is used the most and with what particular subjects or situations.

Example 2: A student, Joan, is presented a story about a red flower. The student visually looks at the word (Ve). She turns her attention inward and makes a visual internal picture of a red flower (Vi). She then attaches an internal feeling to the image (Ki). The learning pattern is Ve-Vi-Ki.

When the student is asked about something she has read, she looks up (Vi visual, internal). Next, she looks down to her right (Ki—kinesthetic, internal) and speaks (Ae), looks up to the left again (Vi—visually remembers), then looks down again to her right (Ki—kinesthetic, internal), as she tells you the story. This is an effective way for this student to remember what she has read.

In listening to her predicates, the teacher can hear her say, "I see ... in my mind's eye (Vi) and I can feel it happening (Ki)." The learning pattern is Vi-Ki. Notice the similarity between the eye movements and the predicates. Observing the learning patterns and recording them over several occasions helps the teacher to identify this student's preferred and most effective pattern for remembering and telling about reading material. Once the teacher determines the student's most effective learning pattern, it can be brought into her awareness in order to increase effectiveness in learning other material.

NOTE: The teacher might also extract effective learning patterns from other students, try them with this student, and compare the learning patterns to determine which is the most effective pattern for this particular student.

LEVEL IV: HOW TO ELICIT A STUDENT'S LEARNING PATTERN

In addition to mapping or recording a student's learning pattern by observing and matching predicate patterns and eye movements, the teacher will now be taught to extract a student's effective learning pattern. This is elicited by asking the student direct questions about the student's behavior. These questions will trigger representations and patterns from the student's history.

In one example, Billy, a student, is met by the teacher for the first time. He is having difficulty memorizing the multiplication tables. In testing the student, the teacher finds that he has learned basic addition so well that he earns 100% on basic addition tests. The teacher must determine what the student did successfully that enabled him to learn the basic addition facts so well. When this learning pattern for learning basic addition facts is determined, the student will be taught to use this same pattern for learning multiplication facts. The following process will be followed:

Teacher:	Establishes rapport with the student.
Teacher:	"Billy, can you tell me about a time when you were able to do some part of arithmetic well?"
Billy:	"Hmmm. I learned my addition facts to 100 well." (Eyes went up to the observer's right.)
Teacher:	"How did you learn them so well?"
Billy:	"I'm not sure. I just studied them." (Eyes move upward and to the observer's right.)
Teacher:	"How did you study them?"
Billy:	"My father held them up on flash cards, and I looked (Ve) at them, then said (Ae) them. He then took them away, and I'd picture (Vi) them as I wrote (Ke) them down. I really don't know how I learned them."

Even though Billy does not consciously understand how he learned basic addition facts, the process is easily observed. His learning pattern is Ve-Ae-Vi-Ke. By listening to his predicates and watching his eye movements, his learning pattern for learning basic addition has been extracted.

It would seem that a simple duplication of this pattern would provide an effective means for the student to learn multiplication. However, Billy's father has left the family, so his mother or another student must hold up the flash cards. Ideally, the cards are held high and to Billy's left, and he repeats the numbers as he pictures them in his mind. He then writes them down.

TOTE is a process used in effective teaching. The teacher must TEST the student to see what s/he knows, OPERATE by teaching the student with a particular learning pattern, TEST the student to see what has been learned, and then EXIT (stop) when the student has achieved mastery. This process is notated as TOTE for TEST-OPERATE-TEST-EXIT. If the learning pattern tested does not prove effective for learning in a particular subject or area, the teacher must continue exploring learning patterns until an effective one is found. The process is repeated until the student succeeds.

Presented below is a series of guidelines and questions that will help you to elicit a student's learning pattern:

1. Tell the student to think of a time when the student succeeded in doing a similar task.
2. Ask the student what was done at that time that enabled him to do the task.
3. Ask the student what was done at the very beginning.
4. Ask the student what was done next, and then next, etc.
5. Ask the student what happened progressively from beginning to end.

The essence of the above is to code the student's learning pattern and have the student use the same pattern in the new situation. It may be necessary for the student to demonstrate what was done, then the student's pattern can be coded readily.

If the student cannot demonstrate what was done in the past because of location, etc., separate the student's past behavior into small, discreet units that will enable you to analyze the pattern. This can be done by asking questions, such as:

1. What is it like to _____?
2. How did you do _____?
3. What happened before you _____?
4. What happened after that? _____?
5. What did you do then? _____?

Keep using the questions until the pattern evolves. Other questions which can be used include:

6. What did you need to do to _____?
7. What happens when you _____?
8. When was the last time you _____?
9. Has there ever been a time when you could _____?
10. What did you do then? _____?
11. What was different then as compared to now? _____?
12. What do you need to do? _____?

The questions asked must be fitted to the individual student and situation. The important principle is to break down the behaviors into small, discreet units and record the learning pattern.

Use the concept of learning patterns with students who have learning problems or with any student who wants to excel at learning something. Examples of student learning patterns are described below. Analyze the pattern, then compare your answers at the end of this chapter. Do **not** proceed until you have mastered these exercises.

Example 1: The student looked at a page of print, then subvocalized what was read. She motorically carried out the experiment she had just read. What was her learning pattern for this activity?

Example 2: The student watched the teacher demonstrate a gymnastics move. The student looked upward to the right and reran the gymnastic move in his mind. The student then went to the parallel bars and tried the move. At the end of the move, he stated, "That didn't feel right!" The student then repeated the process and, at the end, said, "There now, that feels right." What was the learning pattern for this activity?

Example 3: A student in the same class as in Example 2 watched the teacher and made the movements with the teacher as the teacher went through each movement. As the student moved through it, she verbally described what she was doing. She knew she had the entire routine correct when she could silently repeat the sequence to herself. What was the learning pattern for this activity?

ANSWERS: Example 1 - Ve-Ai-Ke
             Example 2 - Ve-Vi-Ke-Ki
             Example 3 - Ve-Ke-Ae-Ai

Chapter 7
Extracting Efficient Learning Strategies or Learning How To Learn

ADVANCED ORGANIZER

OVERVIEW

This chapter will enable you to extract efficient learning strategies from successful learners, and install them in students who have deficit learning systems or learning strategies. Many students academically perform poorly because they have inefficient strategies for learning. If these students are not taught how to study and to learn more effectively, they will continue to perform far below their learning levels. By using this technique, the teacher will be able to help many students to reach far greater achievement levels than either the teacher or student ever thought possible.

CONCEPTS

Belief Negation—Replacing a student's belief concerning inadequate ability with a more positive belief concerning personal ability. For example, a student with a long held belief of inadequacy in connection with academic activities may be re-educated in a positive belief system regarding personal ability, skills, and potential.

Belief Systems—Internal states of expectation concerning future success or failure. For example, a student who has failed some part of arithmetic may believe that she cannot do arithmetic. She has also heard her parents say that girls do poorly in arithmetic. In the future, this belief system may predispose her to do poorly in arithmetic.

Injunctions—A verbal direction or command made by others which serves to install or reinforce belief systems that affect behavior. The statements may be true or false and may serve to set positive and/or negative expectations in the individual. For example, a teacher consistently interjects positive statements (injunctions) while interacting with a student. These positive injunctions may serve to modify the student's future behavior. Unfortunately, negative injunctions also may serve to modify behavior, but in a manner that may minimize performance.

Neurological Physiology—Posture, voice quality, and other aspects of a person's physical being that are directly related to performance. A variable that serves to influence the imitation or modeling of a successful behavior. For example, a student who is a good reader usually sits up straight and holds the book up on the desk. A poor reader tends to slump down in the chair and to place the book flat on the desk. Teaching a poor reader to model a good reader's physiological habits and traits usually will facilitate skills in reading speed and comprehension.

Re-education—A process by which an individual learns to reconstruct or modify an existing belief. A teacher or parent is a vital part in the re-education process. Attention to how and why belief systems are established is necessary if effective re-education is to occur. For example, it may take a teacher many months to overcome the effects of one negative injunction that has established a belief system that is counterproductive to effective learning.

Strategy—The nature and sequence of an individual's utilization of representational systems. Studies on strategies are designed to facilitate and improve learning. For example, good spellers consistently utilize the visual representational system with the auditory representational system as a back up. A poor speller can be taught to imitate this strategy and thus, acquire greater skill in spelling.

VOCABULARY

Phonics—A specific area of linguistics that deals with sounds and their relationship to symbols.
Internal Check—An inner feeling that something is correct or wrong.
Programmed—Internal and/or external sequencing of behavior that is established within an individual.

EXTRACTING EFFICIENT LEARNING STRATEGIES OR LEARNING HOW TO LEARN

As with any instruction, the teacher must identify the specific skill or area to be taught. Students (or others) who perform efficiently and well in that particular skill, knowledge, or content area are then identified. Such students should be able to perform the identified task efficiently and with ease. It is best to begin by observing and studying several students who perform the task well and with ease.

The next step is to analyze the student and academic task in terms of basic areas of learning:

1. Neurological physiology
2. Strategy
3. Belief systems
4. Feelings and emotions.

In the following discussion, an academic skill or task will be examined with respect to these four basic areas. The differences in the learning patterns of a good speller and a poor speller will be compared. What they do and how they learn will be extracted and discussed in terms of the above four basic areas.

NEUROLOGICAL PHYSIOLOGY

First, the teacher should observe the neurological physiology of good spellers. Good spellers often sit erect or stand straight when they are spelling. Voice tonality is high and even. Their bodies are relaxed, shoulders down, and their heads are straight and up, with foreheads smooth. The teacher should observe the neurological physiology of poor spellers. Poor spellers often sit poorly in a hunched-over position. Voice tonality may vary in volume and pitch. Their bodies are tensed, and their chins are close to their chests. Their foreheads are often wrinkled and their eyes move everywhere, rarely maintaining a steady or fixed gaze.

All of these physiological aspects affect learning. Imagine trying to catch a high fly ball with your head down and the palms of your hands extended outward. The ball is not likely to be caught because the optimal functioning and coordination of the eyes and hands are not being activated. What poor spellers do is similar in that their physiology is not coordinated or conducive to spelling words correctly.

It is important to remember that our total being is always involved in learning. The better the teacher understands how all the parts are interrelated in effective learning, the more efficient both teaching and learning will become.

STRATEGY

There are many ways to extract strategies. For the purposes of simplicity, eye strategies will be explored. In observing good spellers, the teacher will notice that they look up and to the observer's right or straight ahead and defocused as they spell words. These students picture the words before spelling them. Picturing a word is a more accurate method of spelling words as compared to sounding them out.

Students who win spelling contests know that a large percentage of English words cannot be spelled phonetically. Consider the word "phonics" itself. If "phonics" were spelled phonetically, it would be spelled "fonix". In a spelling bee, "fonix" would be considered incorrectly spelled, although it is phonetically correct. An amazing number of students misspell the words "many" and "come" on standardized achievement tests. "Many" is often spelled "meny" and "come" is often spelled "kom". A study by Van Nagel (1984) showed that 36% of the words missed by elementary students in one school district were words that could not be correctly spelled phonetically.

Observing students who spell poorly, the teacher may notice that the student's eyes go down or to the right or left as they spell (see Illustration 8). Their eyes often shift back and forth from ear to ear, left to right, right to left, rather than looking up to their left, as in the case of a good speller. Usually, when a poor speller's eyes shift, it indicates that the student will misspell the word. There are three possible explanations for the misspelling. The authors hypothesize that, after students shift their eyes, they shift from one neurological system of the brain to another neurological system of the brain. The information the student needs may, or may not, be stored in the part of the brain being accessed. The eye shifting itself may cause misspelled words.

Good spellers tend to look up and to their left (see Illustration 9). They usually focus their attention there, keeping their eyes in that particular area. These actions help to fix the visual image of the word. Good spellers also have an internal kinesthetic check— hey seem to know when they have spelled the word correctly. They often have feelings associated with correctness. Poor spellers also often know when they have misspelled a word, and they usually respond that they "felt it." Almost everyone has a system of checking. This system is usually an internal system.

Eye strategies are extremely important in both identifying learning and increasing efficiency. Thus, the teacher would do well to practice as much as possible in this area. The following suggestions are given for practice:

1. Keep words written on chalkboard (high and to the left of the room).
2. Have the students write their spelling words on flash cards.
3. Encourage the students to record the words in their memories by taking a picture of the words, then closing their eyes and making sure the words are stored in their mind's eye.
4. Have spelling bees. Pay attention to eye movements of each student as words are spelled. Determine from the eye movements whether or not words are being seen visually as part of the spelling process.

GOOD SPELLERS . . .

Step 1:
See the words.

Step 2:
Check internally--
does it feel right?

Illustration 8

POOR SPELLERS . . .

Step 1:
Sound it out.

Step 2:
Check it out.

Illustration 9

BELIEF SYSTEMS

Traditional educators frequently overlook students' belief systems, thinking that belief systems are better left to the individual and the home. However, belief systems are critical and central to efficient learning. For example, ask good spellers about their experiences with spelling and learning. Listen to their perceptions and beliefs about their spelling ability and about themselves from the perspective of others as well as themselves. They often reflect positive experiences and positive images. When asked specifically about their spelling, they exude confidence in their comments.

These comments and images are recorded in their subconscious minds and influence their belief systems. In effect, these students believe they spell well because 1) they have experienced successes with spelling; and 2) others have told them that they spell well.

In contrast, ask poor spellers about their experiences with spelling and learning. Poor spellers tend to make many negative comments and statements about their spelling abilities and experiences, both from the perspective of themselves and from that of others. These negative comments and images are recorded in their subconscious minds and actually program them to fail at spelling. The way in which students talk to themselves is critical in terms of learning. Their belief systems do affect performance.

For example, do you remember the times that your mother or father told you not to spill your milk or water? What happened? Usually, you spilled the milk or water. The parent's comments preceding your performance actually programmed you, via the subconscious, to do what you were not supposed to do. Similarly, when parents, teachers, or significant others tell students (or anyone) that they spell poorly, perform poorly, or cannot do something, this impacts on the subconscious mind and programs the students (and others) to fail.

When students fail, failure is acknowledged by others. These students then verbalize, rehearse, and repeat the failures, thus getting caught in a vicious cycle. Subsequent negative comments are further instructions to the subconscious confirming inability, failure, or non-success.

Students are simply programmed to repeat their performances of failing, which becomes a self-fulfilling process. Sometimes, merely bringing attention to the negative aspects of learning or doing a task creates a mental picture or internal auditory stimulus that can program the subconscious to bring about that event. The younger the student, the more probable the programming.

It is of critical importance that the teacher pay attention to communications with students. Words can create pictures, verbal or auditory reruns, or feelings. Any or all of these can hinder the learning process. The teacher must also be aware of students' internal tapes, or what students tell themselves.

Students do not have to repeatedly experience particular incidents of failure in order to instill negative beliefs about themselves. Repetitive thoughts and associations may strengthen negative programming, thus perpetuating a single negative incident, situation, or thought and reinforce it as if it were an absolute truth. A change in programming can and will make a critical difference in both perception and productivity.

Educators have the responsibility of reprogramming students' negative belief systems, of negating and neutralizing negative programming, and instilling positive, productive programming. Students' belief systems must enable students to learn efficiently and with ease. This can be accomplished by extracting positive programs and belief systems from successful students, and instilling these in less successful or deficient students. (See previous chapter.) Negative belief systems can be neutralized by several means, including belief negation and re-education training.

BELIEF NEGATION

In the strategy of belief negation, the teacher proves to the student that the student can do something that s/he previously thought was not possible, e.g., spell a particular word. The teacher first implants the idea that, in studying and working with the student, the teacher knows that the student has the potential to learn to spell words correctly. To prove the point, the teacher tells the student s/he will help the student learn how to correctly spell a word that the student has previously been unable to spell correctly. The teacher acts and talks with confidence. The student is given a word to spell that s/he has been unable to spell.

Using the effective strategies for spelling described in Chapter 8, the student will be taught how to spell the word. The teacher tells the student s/he knew s/he could spell the word because s/he is now using more of her/his brain power. The teacher points out that the student's brain power has always been there, but the student simply had not learned how to use it correctly and efficiently. The more the student uses this brain power, the more efficient the student's learning will become.

As the student experiences more satisfaction and success, the teacher notes physical and verbal cues and anchors those feelings by pressing a "magic spot" on the student's body. This anchor enables the teacher to trigger that positive feeling for future learning. The student can also use that spot to put her/himself into a positive state for learning in the future. The student is repeatedly told that s/he has the resources to learn whatever needs to be learned.

In this belief change approach, the teacher must remember to provide the student with an experience that negates the failure belief system. The student is consistently and repetitively given the message that s/he can learn. Spelling is only one of many mediums that can be used to change a negative belief system.

RE-EDUCATION TRAINING

Another strategy that can be used to change the student's belief system is re-education training. Re-education training is based on the principle that thinking processes are the result of a repetitive pattern consisting of what a person has been told to believe, or what a person has told her/himself to believe. For example, many female students have often been told (or have heard) at an early age that females are not as good as males at doing arithmetic. They have repeated this thought to themselves as well as to others. As a result, these females have continued to believe that they cannot do arithmetic well, or cannot do it as well as males. Thus, these females have programmed themselves, both consciously and subconsciously, not to perform as well in arithmetic as they actually are capable of doing.

With this negative framework, any mistakes made in arithmetic serve to strengthen the belief that they have reduced capability and productivity in arithmetic. Attention is focused subconsciously on mistakes rather than successes. Their negative belief systems affect their thought processes and, consequently, their performances. This is shown below:

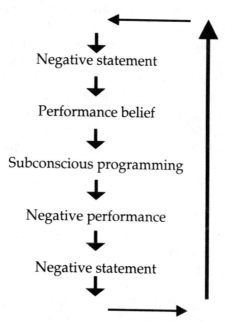

Negative statement

Performance belief

Subconscious programming

Negative performance

Negative statement

This vicious cycle must be broken if productive, efficient learning is to be accomplished.

INJUNCTIONS

The cycle described above can be broken with the constant repeating or reprogramming of positive injunctions. An injunction is a direction or command. By the use of positive injunctions, a negative belief system (such as the one above) can be neutralized or changed.

When talking to students, teachers should accent statements in their conversations that affirm tasks well done by students. A comment may be made on how arithmetic is becoming easier for the student. The intention of the teacher is to gracefully and unobtrusively reprogram the student's subconscious mind with a positive belief system about learning arithmetic. This may require many repetitions of the injunction, plus constant reassurance to the student of her/his ability to do the task.

Specifically, the teacher might say, "I noticed how nice it has been outside today, and I heard that the weather is going to continue to be nice." The student nods in agreement, as the teacher continues, "I corrected your arithmetic papers and I noticed that you finished all of your problems." Again, the student nods in agreement and says, "I did." The teacher then states, "Arithmetic is getting easier for you. As time goes on, you will find it even more enjoyable and easier for you. You may even want to study it more and more." The teacher's voice emphasizes the underlined words, so as to reprogram the student's belief system. The effective teacher will utilize injunctions frequently and subtly. Change may not always occur with only a few injunctions.

The teacher must be tactful and find ways to make injunctions as unobtrusively as possible. Positive injunctions must be repeated to the student until they become part of the student's belief system. Because the subconscious functions in a literal sense, it accepts whatever is stated as truth. Therefore, as injunctions are repeated in different ways by the teacher, the student finds that s/he actually does enjoy arithmetic. The student's belief system changes from a negative one to a positive one. In essence, this is a form of motivation.

FEELINGS

Feelings can either facilitate or hinder the learning process. Feelings are rooted in past experiences of success or failure. If a student has good feelings about learning or a subject, s/he will be motivated to learn that subject because of the past pleasant associations. By the same token, if the student has unpleasant feelings about learning or a subject, s/he will tend to avoid learning about that subject.

When students have negative feelings about learning, the techniques of collapsing anchors, change history, and disassociation discussed previously should be used to nullify these unpleasant feelings. Equally as important, the teacher should use the information contained within this book to program the student in the area the student has negative feelings.

Remember these key points:

1. Start instruction at the student's level of success.
2. Break instruction into small sequential steps.
3. Constantly reinforce the student's efforts and successes.
4. Call attention to the student's progress.
5. Review regularly.
6. Point out how the new information can be used in the student's life.
7. Associate past positive experiences with the new information to be learned.

EXERCISE

PURPOSE: A guide for extracting a strategy.
DIRECTIONS: Find three persons who do something well without effort. Use the Steps for Assessment as outlined below to extract the strategy of each person. Utilizing this information, duplicate the performance of the three people you have selected.

1. **Physiology**
    Eye position
    Body posture
    Breathing
    Movement or nonmovement
    How does the person attend or concentrate?
    What enables the person to concentrate?
    How? What?

2. **Strategy**

    What do you do first?

    What do you do next?

    How do you get it? Chunk down levels and task analyze.

    Show me by imitation.

3. **Belief System**

    What is your belief on learning?

    How was your belief acquired?

    When was your belief acquired?

    What makes you believe it now?

    How often do you tell yourself or someone else that belief?

4. **Feeling**

    What do you feel?

Chapter 8
Learning Strategies
Of High Achievers
For Spelling, Arithmetic,
And Reading

ADVANCED ORGANIZER

OVERVIEW

In this chapter, you will learn how to rapidly increase student learning and achievement in spelling, arithmetic, reading, and writing. This information is based on elicited strategies of students and adults who easily perform at high levels in these particular content areas.

At this writing, 527 persons have been studied and their strategies have been extracted and coded. Common elements in the strategies of high achievers have been extracted and recorded. From this data, a body of information has been synthesized and tested on various individuals.

The authors now offer to you, the teacher, efficient elements and strategies of successful learners that can be taught to most students. The strategies described here have been applied to many students, most of whom have demonstrated significant increases in academic performances. In the authors' opinions, those students who were taught the strategies and did not improve significantly were in need of intensive Neurolinguistic Programming due to specific negative conditioning and emotional problems. The authors continue to research this area and will soon be publishing the results.

It is important that the teacher use the information in this chapter in conjunction with the information in the preceding chapters. Application of these techniques without the use of rapport, calibration, etc., renders them less effective.

In presenting this chapter, the focus will be on what rapid learners and high achievers do when learning spelling, arithmetic, reading, and neat handwriting skills. (Future editions will focus on study skills and advanced subjects.) The information will be chunked into four components to facilitate comprehension. The components to be described in each subject area are: Physiology, Strategies, Belief Systems, and Feelings.

CONCEPTS

Strategies of High Achievers—Techniques of physiology, belief systems, strategies, and feeling states that have been extracted from a person who does a task well and without effort.

Teacher's Self Check Sheet (to monitor spelling program)—An inventory of desirable teacher and instructional behavior designed to facilitate correct spelling.

Chunks/Chunking—Specific information that represents a grouping of the total task. For example, when spelling a word, most students will pause after spelling several letters of a word. This represents a chunk. In a division problem, the first step of dividing 242 by 2 is 2 into 2. This represents a chunk. When you remember your telephone number, it is usually chunked by three numbers for the area code, three for the prefix, and four for the remainder.

LEARNING STRATEGIES FOR HIGH ACHIEVEMENT IN SPELLING

The spelling elements that good spellers use when spelling words will be outlined. It is suggested that the teacher first try the strategy with one student. Strategies learned in prior chapters will need to be modified according to individual student needs until the student's optimal learning level is reached. To begin, select a student and follow the procedures described below.

NEUROLOGICAL PHYSIOLOGY

Proper posture and body alignment promote more effective learning. Instruct the student to sit up straight and to sit still.

Voice tonality, voice tempo, and breathing affect both communication effectiveness and emotional state, e.g., receptivity, anxiety, etc. Tell the student to use a voice tonality that is moderately high and steady.

Adjust the student's speech until it has an even tempo. Do this by practicing spelling words together. The student will model your speech tonality and tempo. Tell the student to adjust his/her breathing pattern, so that it is rhythmic and smooth.

STRATEGY

There are many strategies that may be used in promoting high achievement and optimal learning. The strategy for spelling is as follows.

Step 1—Show the student a total of five different pictures, one at a time. After showing the student one picture for five seconds, remove it, and ask the student to describe what was seen in the picture. Notice the first eye movement of the student for this picture and for each subsequent picture.

Step 2—Ask the student to identify a favorite hero, heroine, or object. Tell the student to picture the spelling words about to be taught on the hero, heroine, or object. Make sure the person or object the student has selected is clear in the student's mind.

Now show the spelling word that is to be learned to the student. Hold the card to the upper left of the student. Instruct the student to look in the same direction used for remembering and describing the pictures.

Tell the student to look in that direction and picture the word being learned on the favorite hero, heroine, or object, as though it were tattooed or engraved on the person or object holding the word selected.

Step 3—If the student seems to have difficulty with the word due to its length, break it into manageable chunks. The teacher can determine how much of a chunk (number of letters) a student can comfortably handle at one time by the number of letters handled before pausing.

Step 4—First, have the student spell the word backward. This forces the student into a visual processing mode. (This is the processing mode most used by students who win spelling bees. According to Hanna and Hammil [1980], many English words cannot be spelled phonetically, so a visual learning mode is more effective in learning to spell.)

Now, have the student see the word on a favorite hero or object and spell it forward.

Step 5—When teaching the student a new spelling word, try manipulating the following variables to see if it improves the student's correct recall of the word. Students will vary, so it is important that the teacher experiment with these techniques.

a. While looking at the word and picturing it on the forehead of a favorite hero, heroine, or object, have the student increase the size of the word. (Also, try decreasing the size of the word.)

b. As the student pictures the word, have the student brighten or darken the word. When the student is recalling the letters, have the student brighten the entire picture around the word.

c. While teaching the word to the student, vary the physical distance of the printed word and note its effect on retention. Move it closer or further from the student's eyes until you find the optimum distance for the student.

d. If the student's eyes shift while spelling a word, have the student return to the original eye position. This is important for storing and retrieving the information in the brain.

e. Have the student trace and say the word as it is pictured on the favorite hero, heroine, or object. Try this first by having the student **picture,** then **trace** the word. Next, try having the student **picture, trace,** and **say** the word. Compare the approaches to find the one that is most effective for the student.

BELIEF SYSTEM

Belief systems are the foundation for optimal learning, as attitudes, thoughts, perceptions, and actions evolve from the individual's belief system. Thus, it is important that the student have a positive, constructive belief system rather than a negative, nonconstructive belief system.

Tell the student that the method you are about to teach is a new foolproof method based on special psychology. Inform the student that, as the system is learned, the ability to remember spelling words correctly will improve at a rapid rate.

If the student uses words or phrases such as "I can't spell," **immediately** stop the student and have the student repeat three times, "I **can** spell!" Use the belief change strategies outlined in the previous chapter to change negative, counterproductive strategies to positive, productive strategies.

FEELINGS

As stated before, a positive emotional state is a significant component to optimal learning. Negative feelings can be a real impediment to learning. ERASE THEM! If the student has unpleasant feelings associated with spelling, use the procedure for collapsing anchors as described previously. Also, if negative feelings about past events or situations are affecting the student's learning, use the appropriate change techniques to promote an emotional state more conducive to learning. Help the student to establish and maintain positive feelings.

LESSON PLANS

A step-by-step weekly lesson plan for spelling follows the

basic procedure as described above. Be sure to adjust the weekly lesson plan to individual student differences and learning levels. This approach to teaching spelling has proven far superior to traditional methods. The procedure should be followed closely and consistently to reach maximum spelling achievement. Teachers should read the entire procedure **before** teaching spelling. Thereafter, the outline of each day's activity should be followed consistently. Spelling words can be taken from the sources used throughout the day, thereby integrating the spelling activity with other activities. More difficult words may be taken from science and history texts. This also helps to teach word meanings.

As teachers use this system, they will find that their students' abilities to spell words correctly rapidly increase over a three to four week period. This approach has worked very well with students labeled "learning disabled" and "mildly mentally retarded." Average students have become superior spellers with this approach. In addition, visual memory of both teachers and students improves with use of this approach. This new approach can be exciting for both teachers and students!

For purposes of direction and clarification, specific examples, exercises, and lesson plans are described in the following pages.

PHASE A: PRE-ASSESSMENT

1. Identify and select a group of five to ten words you will be teaching the students.
2. Calibrate the student's eye movement patterns as they are related to visually remembered by showing the student five pictures. Present each picture individually and hold in student's sight for five seconds.
3. The picture is then removed from the student's sight and the student is asked to describe the picture.
4. Observe the direction of the student's first eye movement. Make a copy of the neurological face map in Appendix 4. Place a check mark in the box that indicates the direction of the student's first eye movement for each picture. For example, the teacher presented five pictures, one at a time, to Karen. She looked at the first picture for five seconds. The

teacher removed the picture and asked Karen to describe the picture. Karen's first eye movement was up and to her left. A check mark was placed in the box indicating the direction of her eye movement. The teacher followed this process in presenting each of the pictures. For each of the five pictures, Karen's initial eye movement was up and to her left. Karen's eye movement pattern for accessing visually remembered material was up and to her left.

If further verification is desired, ask the student the following questions, using the neurological face map in Appendix 4. Mark an X in the box that correlates to the direction of the student's first eye movement in response to the following questions:

1. What does your bedroom look like?
2. What does your mom's (or dad's) hair look like in the morning?
3. What does your favorite movie or television star look like?
4. What color is your favorite animal?
5. Make a picture in your mind of the things you like to do (or your favorite dessert).

PHASE B: INSTRUCTIONAL

Once you have identified the student's eye pattern movement for accessing visually remembered material, explain to the student that it is easier to remember reading and spelling words when the eye looks in that specific direction. Specifically tell the student that this new method of learning spelling words will facilitate the correct spelling of the word. Affirm the fact that the more this procedure is used, the easier it is to spell words correctly.

Daily plans follow which include directions for teaching spelling to a group of students. Remember to calibrate for individual differences. For students who have a different eye accessing pattern for visual remembered material, modify the direction for them during your presentations.

The following instructions are to be given to students **each**

day during the teacher's pre-instructional phase:

1. Clear everything off your desk.
2. Put your feet on the floor.
3. Sit up straight.
4. All eyes on me.
5. Take a deep breath and let the air out slowly.

DAY 1

Instructions: As you face the chalkboard, write the first five new spelling words in the upper left hand corner of the chalkboard. Always use the same color chalk. Show a picture or an object depicting the word, holding it in the direction of students' eye movement accessing patterns for visually presented material. This is to the students' left. Make sure the meaning of the words is understood. Have the students make sentences using the words. Have the students practice spelling the first five words by doing the following:

1. Tell the students to look up at the word and picture it on the forehead or chest of their favorite hero, heroine, or object. Instruct them to take a picture of it with their "mind's camera eye" and hold it there. Remove the word from view, and move around the room, selecting students randomly to spell words backward, then forward. **Spelling words backward forces the student to make a visual picture of the word.**

2. Direct students to choose a partner across the aisle and hold hands with the partner. The teacher makes sure each student has a partner. The student who does not have a partner is the teacher's partner.

The teacher, raising her/his right hand, stands in front of the class and tells the students that the partner on the right is partner number one. The teacher instructs all the number ones to raise their hands (for verification). The teacher then tells students that the partner on the left is partner number two . All number twos are instructed to raise their hands. The teacher continues with the lesson, having partner number one spell to partner number two. S/he then reverses it, so that partner number two spells to partner number one.

This provides active participation and practice for all students. The teacher circulates and listens to as many students as possible.

3. Assign the first five spelling words for homework. Tell the students to study the spelling words at home and at school, and to use the same method they were taught in school.

DAY 2

Instructions: Give the required daily teacher's pre-instructional phase. Review the previous five spelling words according to the directions given in Day 1. Have the students look up and to their left and picture each word on their favorite hero, heroine, or object. Have them picture it in the same color as clearly as they can picture it. Next, have the students write each spelling word as you dictate it to them. Have the students check the spelling of their words against the correct spelling.

Teach the next five spelling words according to the procedure given for Day 1, and assign the additional five spelling words for homework study.

DAY 3

Instructions: Give the daily required teacher's pre-instructional phase to students. Write several misspellings of each of the five words, along with the correct spelling of words in different places on the chalkboard or on a ditto. Have students mark which words are misspelled. Then do the following:

1. If a student has difficulty identifying the correct spelling, repeat the activity used in Day 1. Tell the student to look at the word and picture it on the forehead or chest of their favorite hero, heroine, or object. Tell the student to take a picture of it

with the "mind's camera eye" and keep this image in the mind. Remove the word from view; move around the room having the student spell the word backward, then forward. Spelling the word backward forces the student to make a visual picture of the word.

2. Give the students a pretest to see which words are misspelled consistently. The teacher should say the word, use it in a sentence, then say the word again.

3. Have the students exchange papers and correct misspelled words for each other. Students checking the spelling papers are to write the correct spelling beside misspelled words. A tally/hand count will identify words misspelled most often.

4. Assign all ten words for homework. Tell the students to study the words at home using the same method they were taught in school. Instruct them to give additional practice time to the words they misspelled.

DAY 4

Instructions: Give the students the daily required pre-instructional phase. Using words determined to be difficult by the previous day's test, write the words in very large letters in the upper left corner of the chalkboard (facing the chalkboard). Divide the word into chunks of three letters each. Have the students look at the words and again picture it in the "mind's camera eye." Have them make the letters brighter on their hero, heroine, or favorite object, and move the "snapshot" or picture closer or further until the letters are very clear. Have the students spell the word backward, then forward.

It may help to have the student spell only part of the basic word, then spell the remaining chunks. The learning of some students will be enhanced by having them trace the word in the air with a finger, and say the word as they spell it backward, then forward. By trial and error, identify which students are helped by one or more of these techniques.

Give the students a pretest by saying each of the ten spelling words. The teacher should say the word, use it in a sentence, and say the word again. Have the students exchange papers and correct each other's words .

Do a tally and find out which words were misspelled most frequently. Assign all ten words for homework. Tell the students to spend more study time on their misspelled words.

DAY 5

Instructions: Give the daily teacher's pre-instructional phase to the students. Give a spelling test using the ten words taught that week. Say the spelling word, then use it in a sentence, then say it again. Remind the students to look up and to their left when remembering to spell the words.

After the test, have the students check each other's papers using their spelling books or spelling lists for the correct spelling. Return the papers and have the students write the correct spelling of the word by each misspelled word.

The students should keep a list of all misspelled words in the back of a folder or tablet. They should practice these words the rest of the period, or until they can spell the words correctly. Students who spelled all the words correctly on their tests can draw or play with puzzles, etc. The students who misspell words should practice them each day until they spell all of them correctly.

FACTORS TO CONSIDER WHEN TEACHING SPELLING

Make sure the students sit straight when they are spelling. Have students breathe high in the chest to enhance the visual process.

If a student consistently misses words when a particular posture, chair, or place is used, move the student to another posture, chair, or place. The student may be conditioned to fail in that particular posture, chair, or place.

Break the word up into syllables and have the student spell part of the word, then additional parts.

When a student shows signs of being fatigued, stop and move to another activity.

Teach the students' parents the strategy and have them review the words with the students every night.

When working with the students, tell them that this is a foolproof strategy and they will learn to spell words easily by this method. Do not permit the student to make such negative statements as "I can't." If the student makes such a statement, insist that the student say, "I **can!**" three times. If they resist or refuse saying "I can," have them try saying, "I used to have trouble with spelling. This is a new and better way to spell." This will help in changing the student's belief system from negative to positive, thereby enhancing learning.

A CHECK SHEET TO MONITOR THE SPELLING PROGRAM

YES NO

___ ___ 1. Spelling words are written on the upper left corner of the blackboard.

___ ___ 2. Teacher shows pictures depicting spelling words.

___ ___ 3. Pictures are used to teach the meanings of the words.

___ ___ 4. Teacher tells students to visualize the words on a favorite person's chest or forehead, and take a picture with the "mind's eye camera."

___ ___ 5. Teacher teaches students to spell backward, then forward.

___ ___ 6. Teacher gives spelling pretest.

___ ___ 7. Teacher assigns words for homework.

___ ___ 8. Teacher reteaches misspelled words.

___ ___ 9. Teacher divides spelling words into manageable letter chunks.

___ ___ 10. Students keep misspelled words in folders and practice them for the rest of the period, while others are involved in other activities.

ACTIVITIES

ACTIVITY 1
Contrast and investigate a good speller and a poor speller in terms of:

Physiology
1. Body posture
   a. Shoulders
   b. Back
   c. Feet
2. Tonality
3. Tempo
4. Breathing

Strategy
1. Eye position/movement
2. Closing the eyes
3. Knowing when it is right
4. Change sensory variables
   a. Increase size
   b. Decrease size
   c. Chunk it
   d. Brighten it
   e. Bring it in closer or push it out further. Try variations.
   f. Focus it

Belief System
1. Check and compare belief systems
2. Change belief system of poor speller

Feelings
1. Good versus bad
2. Calm versus tense

ACTIVITY 2
Have a good speller look down to the right while spelling words. See what happens! The student's spelling efficiency will be impaired.

ACTIVITY 3

Group students who have similar strategies for success. Elicit their strategies and teach these to poor spellers. Simplified spelling strategy steps are:

1. Program belief system to a positive expectation.
2. Identify the student's eye accessing pattern.
3. Teach the student, using the student's identified visual accessing pattern.
   a. Eye position—Student's upper left (in most cases). Show the word and tell the student to take a picture of it (camera example).
   b. Student puts the word on the hero or heroine or favorite object.
   c. Student adjusts the mind similar to a camera, television, or movie e.g., brightness, color, focus.
4. Have student spell the words backward, then forward.
5. Instruct the student to sit straight, not move around (yet be relaxed), and breathe slowly.
6. If failure occurs: Chunk if necessary—use three letter chunks. If it still fails, brighten picture and adjust variables. If no success, check 7 and 8.
7. Check belief system by questioning.
8. Check feeling states by questioning:
   a. A time when student spelled well (anchor).
   b. A time when student did something well (anchor).
   c. What in this is similar to what student already can do?
   d. Pace.
   e. Do not let students say negative things, even to themselves.
   f. Use positive injunctions.
9. Use peer teaching.
10. Use the upper left corner of the chalkboard to place material to be learned.
11. Use future pacing. Tell the student, "From now on, whenever you want to spell this word, you will simply remember this picture in your head and spell the word correctly. "
12. Watch for these interfering behaviors:

a. Too much muscle tension.
b. Eye shifts (shift, brain accessing), thus interfering with retrieval.
c. Fatigue—If the student is tired, stop and take a break.
d. Frustration—When the student is frustrated, choose smaller words or temporarily change the activity.
13. Extra Ideas:
a. Remove negative feelings—by disassociation or the "movie technique. "
b. Calibrate emotions.

STRATEGIES FOR HIGH ACHIEVEMENT IN HANDWRITING

In this section, the teacher will learn effective strategies used by persons who are considered to have excellent handwriting. Criteria for excellent handwriting include five components. These components, listed in decreasing order of importance are: shape of letters, size of letters, spacing of letters, slant of letters, and speed of writing.

We will first consider the neurological physiology of students and others who have excellent handwriting.

NEUROLOGICAL PHYSIOLOGY

Students and others who write well generally place themselves in a stable, comfortable position. Specifically, their feet are flat on the floor, legs are not crossed, the small of the back touches the back of the chair, the back and spinal column are straight, and the head is slightly tilted forward. The authors have noted that whenever the desk or table on which the student is writing is below the waist, the student's handwriting is affected negatively.

Right-handed writers usually grasp the pen or pencil 3/4 inch to one inch above the pen or pencil point. The thumb is across from the first major crease in the index (first) finger. The right little finger and side of the palm/hand rest on the desk or table on which they are writing. The paper is usually slanted at about forty-five degrees to the person.

Left-handed writers who write well usually use the same physiology, except the paper is slanted the opposite direction at about forty-five degrees or almost horizontally to the student. The pen or pencil is held one to one and one-half inches above the pen or pencil tip.

The authors found that good handwriters possess a calm, relaxed internal state, whereas poor handwriters were usually tense, with shoulders elevated, and wrote fast. This appeared to be a critical variable as far as neurological physiology was concerned. When handwriters who normally wrote poorly relaxed, shifted their breathing from upper body to lower body, and reduced their speed of writing, there was a noticeable improvement in their handwriting.

In order to experience this breathing style, place both of your feet flat on the floor, lower your shoulders, and breathe in a slow and rhythmical manner from your stomach area. This type of breathing will henceforth be referred to as learning breathing.

Contrast this breathing with raising your shoulders and breathing from your upper chest area. After having experienced the difference between these two physiological styles, you will find it easier to teach students how to do the same thing.

STRATEGY

Place a student whose handwriting is poor in the correct physiology as described above. Anchor a state of relaxed yet alert calmness in the student. Place this student beside a student whose handwriting is excellent. (Right-handed students should sit next to right-handed students, and left-handed students should sit next to left-handed students.)

Have the poor handwriter model what the good handwriters' do or tell the poor handwriters to pretend they are the teacher while they are writing. Have teacher's samples of excellent handwritten letters taped to the top of the students' desks. The students' best efforts may also be taped to the desks.

At first, the student should trace large, excellent reproductions of the letters. Letters should be two spaces high. The student should remain calm, alert, and relaxed while doing the tracing exercise. The teacher may need to retrigger the relaxation anchor. When the student can do this part well, proceed to the next step.

Have the student make reproductions of the letters below the traced letters two spaces high. When the student can reproduce the traced letters with close approximation, remove the model and have the student do it from memory. When the student can do this accurately, have the student trace letters one space high.

When the student can reproduce the traced letter accurately below the traced letters, have the student do the letters from memory, writing them one space high. When the student can do the letters from memory, the teacher may wish to reduce the size of the letters. The next step is to have the student use the above procedure with words, then sentences.

Because handwriting is an imitation skill, the importance of good letter and word models is critical. Letters, both cursive and manuscript, should be placed or taped strategically on the student's desk. Inform the student that handwriting is judged primarily on its shape, size, spacing, and slant.

For example, the teacher may want to point out to the first and second grade students that the little finger should fit between letters for the correct spacing of letters. It may even help to place masking tape on the pencil to indicate where the index finger and thumb should be placed on the pencil. The authors have found an increase in the rate of correct letter reproductions by having the student study by picturing the letter formations above eye level and to the student's left.

When training the student in this manner, instruct the student to imagine tracing the letter on the forehead or chest of a favorite hero, heroine, or object. Have the student move the dominant arm to trace these very large, imagined letters. Tell the student to trace over the letters in such a way as to leave an impression on the hero/heroine/ object. Instruct the student to imagine this hero/heroine/object on the writing paper, then have the student reproduce the letter or word on the paper. This works extremely well with young students (five to seven year olds and older).

BELIEF SYSTEM

Generally, the teacher will be working with young students when teaching handwriting skills. What students are told about their handwriting at a young age leaves an indelible impression on them. Make sure that praise is given for correct written letter and word reproductions.

Use positive injunctions that convey that their reproductions of letters are becoming more like the letter and word models. Whenever a student is seen making a letter or word reproduction that closely approximates the model letter or word, install a positive injunction, such as, "I told you that you would be able to make good letters and letter words."

Have the students circle the best written letters. When they do this, give attention to and comment on these letters e.g., "I notice your 'p' is right on the bottom line," etc. When students make negative comments about their work or anyone else's work, have them state the opposite of what they have said.

FEELINGS

To develop desirable feelings about handwriting, have the student first trace some favorite letters or words e.g., the first letter of the student's name, hero/ heroine, mother, father, etc. Remember to praise the student for good letter reproductions. Select and cut out the student's best letter/word reproductions and send them to the parent with a gold star or a positive comment.

Do not or focus on poor letter formations. Instead, give attention to correct letter formation, shape, slant, size, and spacing. Good feelings associated with writing at an early age will pay large benefits later. Remember that what you give attention to impacts at the conscious and subconscious levels!

STRATEGIES FOR HIGH ACHIEVEMENT IN ARITHMETIC

In this section, the teacher will learn how to improve basic arithmetic skills of students.

NEUROLOGICAL PHYSIOLOGY

After studying young students, ages five to ten years old, one common denominator that emerged from those who did extremely well in arithmetic was the fact that they had the opportunity to manipulate and compare objects at an early age (e.g., blocks, caps, sticks, pots, pans, etc.). This is understandable because arithmetic is primarily a viso-spatial world, a world of visual comparisons.

If students are not given early experiences in handling, comparing, and judging manipulatory objects, this could affect arithmetic performance negatively at a later time. It is hypothesized that these early experiences provide a neurological foundation for future arithmetic learning.

The authors have noted that young students (ages five through ten years) who learn basic addition, subtraction, multiplication, and division facts rapidly do so by re-imaging them after they have seen them. Their physiology entails sitting up straight, with eyes up. Yet, how many teachers tell students to keep their eyes on their papers. The position of the eyes downward may interfere with a student's optimal learning.

Initial observations and comparisons suggest that effective teachers encourage students to manipulate objects as they learn comparisons and counting. When teaching students of any age to learn addition, subtraction, multiplication, division facts, or mathematical equations, have them sit up straight, relax, and breathe rhythmically and slowly as defined in the previous section (learning breathing). These variables tend to produce a state conducive to learning arithmetic.

STRATEGY

After having the student model or imitate the correct neurological physiology, the teacher is ready to teach the student the following strategies for basic addition, subtraction, multiplication, and division facts. If the basic addition or subtraction facts are not known, teach the student how to figure out the answer by counting. See examples below.

Addition

```
 4 (1 1 1 1)
+3 (1 1)
---
7  (1 1 1 1 1 1)
```

Subtraction

```
 7 (1 1 1 1 1 1 1)
-3 (1 1)
---
4  (1 1 1 1)
```

The student in this step is taught to figure out addition and subtraction by counting.

Multiplication

```
 4     (how many in each set)
x 3    (no. of sets) (1111) (1111) (1111)
----
12
```

The student counts the lines in the multiplier (3) to get the product/answer.

Division

```
3)12  (1 1 1) (1 1 1) (1 1 1) (1 1 1)
           (number of sets)
```

The student counts how many sets of three can be obtained from a total of 12.

Once the student understands how to do the above, the student is then taught to memorize the basic facts in the following manner.

Steps for Teaching Arithmetic

1. Using the model used for spelling (five pictures), find out where the student accesses visually remembered material. For most right-handed students, it will usually be up and to their left. Never take this for granted. Always test to find

where the student accesses visually remembered material.

2. Show the student the math facts to be remembered.

3. Place the facts in the area where the student accesses visually remembered material.

4. Have the student superimpose the facts on a favorite hero/heroine/object.

5. Have the student read the facts to you in the following manner:

The student should say, "Four, joined or   4
added to three, line, is the same as seven."   + 3
Then, have the student read it to you back-   ----
ward. Student says, "Seven, line three, joined   7
or added to four."

6. Now, show the student a flash card with 4 + 3 = and ask the student to supply the missing number. Have the following cards made up:

4	4	( )
+3	+( )	+ 3
----	----	----
( )	7	7

Have the student supply the missing numbers. Once the student can do it visually, have the student do it verbally.

The authors have found that the performance of certain students can be enhanced by having them trace the numbers as viewed in their visually accessing positions. Try adding this variable to see if it enhances the performance of some students. Others may benefit from saying and tracing the arithmetic/fact as they are visualizing it on a favorite hero/ heroine/object. Try different variations until each student's optimal learning level is found.

Once the student can do the fact visually, present it orally. Remind the student to picture it on a favorite hero/ heroine or object as the answer is given. It is important to teach only the number of facts per sitting that the student can handle comfortably.

Make sure that the student understands that the plus sign means "joined" and the equal sign means "the same as." This variable differentiated many students who understood basic math facts from those who did not. Arithmetic has its own language. Many high school students did poorly in arithmetic because they did not know basic arithmetic vocabulary. Students who had mastered the arithmetic terminology usually did well on tests.

The teacher can use the same strategy with the subtraction facts, multiplication facts, and division facts as were used with addition facts. When teaching students these strategies, remember to future pace them. You might say to them, "Whenever you want to remember your math facts, just move your eyes to the same position and picture the fact on your favorite hero/heroine/object." Remember to practice this strategy with your students until the strategy becomes automatic or habit.

Advanced equations can be taught to junior and senior high school students in the same manner as described previously. As students progress up the math skills ladder, they will encounter math problems that require many steps. The authors have found that students can master long or complex multiplication and division facts much faster if the teacher chunks down the information in a chunk size that the student can handle comfortably. Once the teacher has found the appropriate chunk size, the teacher can then use the strategies previously described.

The authors have also found attention and concentration to be a factor among students who do well in arithmetic. They noticed that students who learned arithmetic well usually exhibited a calm, relaxed, focused attention on the math fact to be learned. Their initial impression was that this state facilitates the memorization and learning of math facts and equations. Be sure to have the students do "learning breathing" when doing math.

BELIEF SYSTEMS

Our questioning of students who had learned math quickly revealed students who believed that they could do math well early in their lives. Further questioning revealed that they were told by significant others (parents, teachers, etc.) that they were doing well. Attention was focused on their successes and not their failures.

Students who did poorly were convinced early in life that math was difficult or hard. Many females who did poorly in math stated that they had been told by significant others that math was difficult for females and that they should not expect to do well in math. After hearing this negative injunction, many did not try to learn arithmetic well. These injunctions or statements made to young students have a profound effect on their performance in math. Students should be reassured that math can be learned as simply as anything else. The teacher's reassurance to the students that they can learn the math facts does make a tremendous difference. Tell them that, with your method of teaching, everyone learns math.

Arrange learning math so that the student will succeed. It may be necessary to go back to a skill level at which the student experienced success. Provide instructions at this level until the student believes that it can be done. (See Van Nagel Diagnostic Series, 1983.)

FEELINGS

The authors found that students who learned math quickly and easily had good feelings about math. These students had success with math at an early age. Interestingly, they also saw themselves as being able to do math. These feelings were related to early successes and images of being successful in math.

Students who did poorly in math reported early failure in basic math skills. Particularly conspicuous among this group was the fact that teachers generally gave attention to the students' failures rather than their successes. It is readily noted that belief systems, successes, and feelings are all interrelated.

Pleasant and positive experiences must be provided in math for students who do poorly in this subject. Techniques of change history, disassociation, anchoring, etc., may need to be used in order to elicit positive feelings about math. Feelings play a greater role in learning than most educators would care to acknowledge. Educators are now recognizing and acknowledging the tremendous role that feelings play in learning.

STRATEGIES FOR HIGH ACHIEVEMENT IN READING

In this section, the teacher will learn how to install efficient reading strategies in learning to promote higher levels of reading rates and increased comprehension.

NEUROLOGICAL PHYSIOLOGY

The positioning of the body of students who read rapidly and with good comprehension differs significantly from those who read slowly and with poor comprehension. Conspicuously noticeable was the fact that proficient readers usually propped their books up while slow readers laid their books flat on their desks. Also, many individuals reported that they remembered the material easier if they read it while in bed.

Further questioning of this group of students elicited the fact that, while they were lying in bed, books were held at eye level. The authors found that, by having students raise their books to eye level or above, reading rates and reading comprehension improved. This was not true for all students, but it was true for the majority of students that tried this physiological adjustment. It did improve their reading rates and reading comprehension.

Students who placed their books flat on their desks and to their left, daydreamed more and also reported trouble concentrating on their work. The placement of the books to the students' far left and flat on their desks could create a neurological condition which would access or stimulate the emotional centers of the brain. If this happened, other variables (subvocalization) could interfere with the student's cognitive processing.

Having the book flat on the desk also encouraged students to slump over. The authors observed that the majority of readers who read fast and with good comprehension (80% retention or more), usually sat up straight with their feet flat on the floor. The most proficient readers sat in straight back chairs. Along with sitting up straight, the proficient readers reported that although they needed to sit up straight, they also needed to be comfortable. These students also breathed smoothly and evenly (learning breathing). Poor readers usually slumped in their chairs and their breathing was not rhythmic.

Proficient readers appeared to be in a trance-like state with all their attention directed toward what they were reading. Poor readers were distractible and did not seem to put much effort into reading.

Further questioning of the poor readers revealed that the majority of them felt tired or did not have the energy to concentrate, whereas the good readers felt that they had enough energy. This aspect created many questions. Do poor readers lack energy and, if so, what is the cause? (The authors' future studies will look at the factor of energy very closely.)

Among the proficient readers, the authors found that a certain time of day produced higher rates of reading and reading comprehension. Most of the proficient readers reported that they read best early in the morning or late at night (more about this when we discuss study habits in future books). The two variables that emerged after questioning the students were that proficient readers had more energy in the morning and that there was less noise or distraction late at night. It would appear that energy and freedom from distraction are important variables in the reading process.

A majority of the proficient readers required good lighting. Many of them stated that they preferred light from a light bulb, as compared to fluorescent lighting. Dr. Ott's study (1974) revealed that fluorescent lighting tended to make some students more hyperactive. Fluorescent lighting could work against the reading process.

The authors suggest natural light or traditional light bulbs as sources of light. If one has fluorescent lights, it is suggested that they be replaced with the type of fluorescent lights which duplicate natural light as much as possible. This type of full spectrum fluorescent lighting is now available.

STRATEGIES

One of the most conspicuous variables that differentiated proficient readers from inefficient slow readers was subvocalization. Fast readers rarely subvocalize. In other words, they rarely say the word that they have read. Observations of poor readers revealed that most of these students subvocalized while they read. The rate of reading and reading comprehension of this group of inefficient slow readers was improved by merely having them put the tips of their tongues on the roofs of their mouths. This prevented them from subvocalizing.

Proficient readers read groups of words or sentences. Slow readers read word by word. Questioning revealed that many word by word readers did so because they had to concentrate on not losing their places in reading. The authors found that the use of the finger or a ruler below the words enabled them to devote their energy and concentration to reading words. The speed of the slow reader was enhanced by having them move their fingers faster than they normally read. This improved their rates of reading, but lowered their comprehension temporarily.

The magnificence of the brain to compensate and function at higher levels quickly became apparent. In only one to two weeks of practice, student comprehension not only matched what it had been previously, but had surpassed it. The principle involved in this process is that the eye is a detector of motion. As the eye follows the finger, it picks up the words of print. As an individual moves the finger faster, the individual's eye/brain takes in more information. Attention and concentration are enhanced in the procedure. At first, comprehension may drop, but the potential of the brain is tapped and comprehension increases, matches, and surpasses the level at which it functioned previously.

Proficient readers had different rates of reading for different material read. Inefficient slow readers did not vary their rates. Again, the latter group was improved by teaching them to skim over what they were reading. The authors also encouraged them to push their rates of reading on material for which they would not be held accountable.

This increased rate of reading leisure material rapidly generalized to material for which the student would be held accountable. The important variable for increasing reading speed and varying rates with this group was subject interest and appropriate level of reading material. Vocabulary was another variable that emerged when comparing proficient readers with inefficient slow readers. Proficient readers had good vocabularies, whereas inefficient slow readers had vocabularies below their age, grade, or college level. Reading rate and comprehension was improved with the slow readers by teaching the meaning of difficult words before the students encountered them in print.

Many of the proficient readers seemed to enter a state whereby everything but the material to be read was put out of consciousness. Usually, proficient readers had a calm, alert peacefulness about themselves. Inefficient slow readers appeared fidgety and distractible. When a calm, alert, peaceful state was anchored, reading rate was improved. For more information about this area, obtain the Relaxation Response tape by Van Nagel (1984).

The distance at which students held books from their eyes was also different between proficient readers and slow inefficient readers. Proficient readers held their books fifteen to twenty-two inches away from their eyes, while most inefficient slow readers held their books fifteen inches or closer. You can do a little experiment on yourself and note how distancing of a book affects the number of words your eyes can view. Hold a book close to your eyes and note how many words your eyes can see. Now, hold the book beyond fifteen inches and note how many words your eyes can see. You will immediately understand why holding a book close to one's eyes makes for a slow, inefficient word by word reader.

BELIEF SYSTEM

Most of the proficient, fast readers believed that reading was important and would enhance them. Characteristic statements were, "Reading is important;" "My parents said, 'It's important to me.'" etc. Following this major category of responses were reports that reading provided a way to gain information and pleasure. Proficient readers believed that reading served a purpose and that it could be fun. Most proficient readers reported that their parents read to them as a child. This was also evidenced by many books and magazines in the home. This was in direct contrast to the inefficient readers. The inefficient readers believed that reading was tedious work. Their parents rarely read to them. These same readers believed that they could not read well. They were doubtful that they could be trained to read quickly and efficiently.

The techniques of change history and the belief change strategies reported in the previous chapters worked well with these students to change their negative belief systems to positive belief systems.

FEELINGS

Proficient readers reported feelings of alertness coupled with an identification of the material read. Past success with reading was a common denominator among proficient readers. These readers reported pleasant past associations with reading. These associations revolved around parents and teachers reading the books they enjoyed.

Inefficient slow readers reported that they rarely had people to read to them. They reported that the reading material given to them in school was far above their reading levels and early failures associated with reading gave them negative feelings about reading. These individuals preferred to obtain information and recreation by other means.

The importance of early pleasant associations with reading was replete with reports of proficient fast readers. Parents and teachers are advised to read interesting stories to children and students from the time they are babies. This not only associates pleasant feelings with reading, but also gives the student quality time with the parent. Early pleasant associations of reading to students by parents, teachers, and others were found in the majority of the proficient fast readers.

Sadly, with this information, some young students are not provided these experiences. Nevertheless, the negative feelings that accompany inefficient slow readers can be changed. This can be done with the techniques of change history, collapsing anchors, physiological neurological change, and the other strategies described in the preceding chapters.

Books also can be provided that match the interests and needs of the students. Examination of traditional text books and their use in schools today reveals that they often lack relevancy to the student. Students do not care about reading materials that are not relevant to their present model of the world.

Forcing a student to read dull, drab, irrelevant materials that have no perceived purpose or utility will soon bring about negative associations with reading. This, coupled with the readability levels that fluctuate beyond the majority of most students in the junior and senior high school levels, undoubtedly is setting the stage for failure and negative associations. The amount of reading required of students in some secondary schools is overwhelming. It appears that teachers expect students to learn mostly from reading, rather than from teaching.

Teachers constantly tell students to study, but they do not teach them how to study. Teachers must teach students how to study. Learning can be made enjoyable by using the powerful tools suggested in this chapter. Practice and apply these techniques and you will be delighted with the resulting high achievement.

Chapter 9
Teaching Students To Use Their Inner Resources For Unlimited Potential

ADVANCED ORGANIZER

OVERVIEW
In this chapter, you will learn to teach your students methods of eliciting strategies of competent people. Once your students have elicited and incorporated effective strategies, they can use them successfully in one context and then transfer the knowledge to other contexts. The final area to be addressed is the ability to internally generate creative strategies and solutions.

CONCEPTS
Limitation—The internalized belief system that directs individuals to concentrate on limitations rather than on possibilities and assets. For example, most individuals dwell on what they cannot do rather than what they can accomplish.

Modeling—The extraction and imitation of strategies of an individual, who is able to perform a task extremely well and seemingly without effort.

Creative Synthesis—The combining of two or more strategies to effect a more powerful outcome. Example: Employing modeling and visualization to learn a new sport skill.

VOCABULARY

Presupposition—The fundamental beliefs upon which a theoretical approach is based.

Inner Resource—The resources stored within the experiences of an individual that can be brought to another or a new context.

Internal Tape—The replay of memories of yourself or others. They can be positive or negative.

Internal Visualizations—The process of seeing an image in the mind's eye.

TEACHING STUDENTS TO USE THEIR INNER RESOURCES FOR UNLIMITED POTENTIAL

In Neurolinguistic Programming, the basis of the ideas in this book, there is a presupposition that an individual has all the resources necessary to make any desired change. If this presupposition is taken literally, the question could be raised, "Are they saying that if I lost an arm, I could grow a new one back?" The answer to this question, in the context of the present knowledge, is obviously "No." In the genetic code, there exists all of the information that would be needed to regenerate an arm if we knew how to tap it. Perhaps within the next twenty years, genetic researchers will make this type of breakthrough.

There is another way of viewing the idea of unlimited resources within us. A number of studies have shown that some selected individuals with superior I.Q.'s had massive brain tumors that should have destroyed their ability to perform. After surgery, many of these individuals regained the ability to perform. We do not know what these individual cases mean. However, it certainly does raise questions about what is possible. Both examples are designed to get you, the teacher, to ask the question, "What is possible with my students?" Could it be that more is possible than we have ever imagined before—that, indeed, incredible levels of learning and performance are possible?

Much of our traditional training may have taught us to accept the idea of limitation. A method will now be presented to disprove the limitation concept. The first strategy to teach students is how to move resources from one context to another. This strategy is referred to as contextual shifts.

For example, one of the authors recently had a client who could only relate and be comfortable with people after several alcoholic drinks. When this individual drank, it caused people to withdraw from him. When the individual was asked why it was necessary to drink in order to be friendly, he replied, "This is the way I am!" This parallels the idea of a genetic theory of life. The individual was then questioned about whether he was spontaneous and outgoing in any other context. He quickly replied, "No." When questioned about his work situation, it was discovered that he was a supervisor in a large computer firm. Upon further probing, he indicated that he was quite comfortable and gregarious while in the role of supervisor.

This individual was instructed to have an associated memory of the work situation and to step inside that situation and anchor that inner resource of comfort and gregariousness. He was then asked to imagine the next time he would be in a social situation in which he needed to relate to people. He was instructed to trigger that anchor (comfort and gregariousness), so that it would transfer to new social situations.

In order to make this experience more vivid for you, find an example in which you feel emotionally limited, such as feeling uncomfortable in the presence of an authority figure. Now, find a context when you are able to relate to an authority figure. Now, find a context when you are (or have been) able to relate to an authority figure in a comfortable way. You may be the type of person who says, "I'm never comfortable with authority figures." You also may find an example immediately where your relationship with an authority figure was comfortable. Search in as many possible contexts as possible to find an appropriate resource state. If you examine enough contexts, we are sure you will find the perfect example for you.

Having found the perfect example, go back and associate the memory, anchor it, find an appropriate future scene involving an authority figure, associate it and trigger your anchor of the new resource. Now that you have had the experience of searching your own personal history, you probably have found that you have many more resources than you first imagined possible.

Perhaps you have now found that you do not have the resource in the context you want it. Nevertheless, you at least have identified that resource in some context. It remains for you to transfer that resource to the appropriate area.

You are now ready to teach students how to explore their own histories for needed resources and to be able to teach them how to shift resources from one context to another. As you do this with a few students, you will find that it is increasingly difficult to accept student belief verbalizations of limitations.

Modeling is a second method of eliciting a student's inner resources. For some students, it is difficult to locate the context in which a resource may be stored. Sometimes, it is easier to teach the student how to model someone who already expresses the needed resource. Consider the many amateur athletes that study the best athletes and model their behavior and external physiology. By doing so, these amateur athletes improve their performance significantly.

The imitation of behaviors of competent performers, be they in education, sports, etc., is a valuable resource. This resource can be taught to a student by doing the following:

1. Ask the student to select an individual previously known to demonstrate with ease the desired resource.
2. Have the student interview that person and ask the following questions:
    a. What do you do to get ready?
    b. What do you do first?
    c. What do you do next?
    d. What do you see inside your head?
    e. What do you tell yourself?
    f. How do you feel?
    g. How do you do it, step by step?
3. The student continues to relate to that person as follows:
    a. Let me imitate what you do by standing beside you.
    b. Tell me when I am not doing something you do.
    c. What could I do to be more like you when I do this?
4. Have the student rehearse it.
5. Have the student obtain external feedback.

NOTE: More questions may be necessary, depending on the context of performance and the student.

At first, the student should be taught this questioning strategy with small, discreet units of behavior, such as a dance step, standing before an audience before speaking, desirable behaviors for meeting a person for the first time, etc.

The third approach you will learn is creative synthesis. There are many forms of creativity. We will be emphasizing the process of synthesis in the creative process.

Think for a moment about a time during which you were trying to solve a problem, and you found yourself continuously finding the same answer over and over again. That same answer failed to solve the problem. This experience is usually called "getting stuck." Finally, as you worked at the problem, you found a different answer to the problem. As you think back to this experience, one of the things you will notice is that, at some point, you reached a level of resolution and went beyond your mental block.

How did you accomplish the resolution? Think back to the process you used for solving the problem. You might recognize the fact that you went back into your own personal history and found models that you were successful with in similar problems. You replayed the visual and auditory tapes of these memories in your head, or you watched other people who were successful dealing with the problem and started to apply their strategy to your problem.

As you watched either your own successful internal visualization or those reviewed of successful people, you began to extract common components of success. As you remembered these common components, a new pattern was constructed and the new audio/visual tape was played in your head until you found a successful way of solving the problem. You next made a tape of yourself solving the problem and associated yourself in the tape until you had a feeling that you would be able to do the activity. This ability will occur when your associated internal visualization matches your synthesized visualization. This state may be realized from your own successful resources in combination with other successful people.

This same process can be used by both you and your students when you are " stuck" on a problem . The steps are listed below for your convenience:

1. Identify behavior, behaviors, or process desired.
2. Review your successful resources in other contexts.
3. Review others being successful.
4. Combine the common components of success in an internal visualization.
5. Create an audio/visual tape of you in the associative state which matches the combined successful components in Step 4.
6. Internally run the tape of you succeeding.
7. Check to determine if it creates a positive feeling.
8. Do the activity, or go back to the point at which it broke down and start over.

To illustrate this concept, consider a student who wanted to be a student band director. She was first told to make an internal audio/visual tape of how she would look doing the directing. She was then told to go back to any times that she had been successful in leading a group in another context. She was told to extract what she did and synthesize those common components.

The student was instructed to visualize other successful directors and extract their common behavioral components. She then was told to make an internal audio/visual tape that would be synthesizing her own successes and the successes of others. She was instructed to run and rerun the synthesized tape internally. She was then instructed to run that same tape with her doing the activity in an associated state.

When her feelings became positive and she knew she could complete the activity, she was instructed to externally practice directing a group of people. In this particular instance, the student had to go back and add components of external models five more times before her feelings were positive enough for her to practice before a group.

In summary, this chapter provides you with a way to help students shift in context, to model, and to utilize creative synthesis. Each of these techniques is designed to provide the student with a method for breaking through barriers of learning and belief limitations. With practice and care, these three methods will enable you to provide your students with new ways to get "unstuck" whenever they encounter a barrier. You will also find these three approaches helpful to yourself whenever you feel "stuck"!

Chapter 10
Increasing
Communication
Effectiveness or The
Illusion of Understanding

ADVANCED ORGANIZER

OVERVIEW
In this chapter, you will learn the powerful function of language in determining behavior. You will discover that what one word means to a person is not necessarily what it means to another person. You will also learn specific traps that serve to confuse you and others. An understanding of these concepts will help to explain why there is so much miscommunication. You will be provided with knowledge and skills that will enable you to improve and clarify communication. This will result in better human relations and performance.

CONCEPTS
The Map Is Not the Territory—A phrase used to describe the fact that one person's perception of reality may not be the reality of another person. This is because all persons individually develop their own maps or models of the world from the information received through the individual's senses. Thus, one person may perceive the world differently from other persons because individual sensory systems and past conditionings differ.
Nominalization: Abstract Nouns or Vague Nouns—The chang-

ing of an action verb into a static thought or abstract noun. Example: Mrs. Jones has too much responsibility.

Lack of Reference or Somebody/Something is Missing—The lack of a specific reference as to what specific member or person the speaker is referring. Some of the most often used words are: they, them, school, authority, it, she, he, her, him. Example: They will not understand.

Unspecified Verbs or Vague Verbs that connote a condition without being specific as to how or why. Example: Bill does not like me.

Modal Operators or Must Words that imply a required condition. Example: You must do the problem as the teacher told you.

"All the Time Foolers" or Overgeneralization—This occurs if a person generalizes from a few persons, experiences, events, or time sequences to all-inclusive persons, experiences, events, or time sequences. Example: Parents are old-fashioned.

Fortune Telling or Mind Reading—This occurs if one individual thinks she can tell what another individual is thinking. Example: I know you won't agree with me.

Cause and Effect or This Causes That—There is an implication that a relationship to an outcome exists where one does not necessarily exist. Example: If you have good grades, you will get a job.

Lost Performatives or Moral Judgments—When value judgments are placed on behaviors. Example: Changing lesson strategies is bad.

INCREASING COMMUNICATION EFFECTIVENESS OR THE ILLUSION OF UNDERSTANDING

Our common culture has implicitly taught us that language is a clear descriptive way of presenting ideas and facts. Perhaps nowhere in our culture is there such uncritical agreement among people as in the area of understanding the meaning of language. It is almost as if we have made an unwritten agreement with each other that we know what each word represents to each one of us.

If you were to use the word "love" in a sentence, such as "I really love you, John," rarely would anyone stop and ask you what you mean by the word "love." If you asked one hundred people what they meant by the word "love," you would receive one hundred different descriptions and definitions. In fact, if you asked a hypothetical group this question, not only would you receive different definitions, but you would find that people reference the word "love" in many different ways. Some people reference the word to themselves and define love in terms of how they are loving. They may go on to describe the qualities that they have when they are being loving. Others may reference love by describing what other people need to exhibit in order to be loving.

The processing of words provides the illusions and the paradox in which human beings find themselves entangled. On one side of the illusion, we are caught in the assumption that we know what words mean when others say them to us. This provides us with a basic frame of reference, so that communication can run smoothly and so that we can exchange ideas without having to stop and define each word. On the other side of the illusion, each one of us has given our own specific reference to the meaning of particular words. In addition, the English language has hundreds of words that are ambiguous. We need contextual references as well as specific contexts to understand the meaning of a specific word.

THE MAP IS NOT THE TERRITORY

It is important at this point to begin to explore a presupposition in NLP: "The Map is Not the Territory." That is to say that words do not represent true reality (Korsybski, 1933). This presupposition explains how human beings process and store data. At age two or three, you began to hear people use the word "house." As a child, you learned that the word "house" meant your own house. You probably had an internal auditory voice that said the word "house."

A few years later, you learned that the word "house" meant the houses of relatives and friends as well as your house. You then began to record other internal visual images of their houses. By the time you reached school, you probably had several images of houses that you could scan to be able to make sense of the word "house." As you advanced in school, and learned how to read and spell, you probably formed a visual image that was generalized to encompass many houses. Perhaps your image was an image of the house that you presently live in, or the house in which you lived until you left home. It might be a combination of the images of many houses. The generalization that you have formulated for the word "house" will be quite different than that of almost anyone else in the world.

When we move from a concrete object like a house to an abstract concept like trust or love, we begin to grasp the difficulty of communication. Concepts like love and trust tend to move from a specific situation to a generalization that represents an entire class of information. Both the concrete concept of house and the abstract concepts of love or trust are taken from a specific reference point, then generalized to many situations and experiences.

This type of communication can result in ambiguities which, in turn, can lead to errors and problems in communication. Without precise communication, our efforts to communicate, teach, and modify or change behavior are greatly hampered. This chapter will provide you with communication concepts that will greatly enhance your ability to work effectively and efficiently with students and staff.

If you think about where most of your problems in life come from, they come from what you say, how you say it, and what is said to you. Often, the meaning we intend to convey is not interpreted by others the way we intended it to be interpreted. To minimize this problem, we offer the following behavioral semantics model, with examples, so that you will be able to refine your communications and the communications of your students.

NOMINALIZATION: ABSTRACT NOUNS OR VAGUE NOUNS

This is a process whereby a person changes a verb which is active in time into a noun which is static in time. A verb is a process word; it suggests active participation. A noun is static and unchanging. In our early education, we learn about abstract nouns, such as good, bad, trust, success, and failure. Yet, we are not taught how to clarify the meaning behind these abstract nouns when others use them.

We will first examine verbs that have been transformed into nouns. Examples of words in this category are failure (from failing), relationship (from relating), decision (from deciding), and perception (from perceiving). In each example, the result is that the action of the verb has been stopped, thus closing the event. By closing the noun event, the speaker has limited the number of options available.

EXAMPLE 1
Student: "I'm a failure."
Teacher: "**How** are you failing?"
Student: "In math, I'm not able to remember my times tables."
Suggested Clarifications—Change the noun back to a verb form. Use **how** or **what**.
Rationale for Clarification Questions—Notice that the student has now **specified the area of difficulty.** The question has reduced the generalization of failure in everything to a specific area. You now have important information about the student's belief system in math. Secondly, you now have a better idea of the area of math in which the student is experiencing difficulty. You can now teach the student how to solve a specific problem. In this case, you will teach memorization utilizing visualization. (Refer to preceding chapters.)

EXAMPLE 2
Student: "I don't have a good relationship with my science teacher."
Teacher: "How is the way you are relating causing problems?"
Suggested Clarifications—Change the noun back to a verb form. Use **how** or **what**.
Rationale for Clarification Questions—When students use nouns as verbs, they are in a closed frame of reference. If you accept a closed event, you limit discussion and problem solving. By changing the noun back to a verb form, you place the student in the role of an active participant. This extends the student's range

of responses and allows for more effective problem-solving.

LACK OF REFERENCES OR VAGUE PRONOUNS

In this category, the speaker omits the specific reference as to what member of a class s/he is referring. This can cause serious communication problems. As a tipoff, watch for pronouns such as he, she, it, they, those, this, her, him, and others.

EXAMPLE 1
Student: "It is the way they treat me that causes me to fail."
Teacher: "**Who,** specifically, causes you to fail?"
Suggested Clarifications—Verbalize the specificity, e.g. "**Who (What) specifically** . . . ?"
Rationale for Clarification: In this example, the teacher gains information by virtue of the clarification question. Once the student identifies who/ what is thought to be causing the problem, further questioning can delineate the perceived area of difficulty.

EXAMPLE 2
Student: "The teachers are unfair to me."
Teacher: "**What specific** teachers are unfair to you?"
Suggested Clarifications—"**What specifically** . . . ?" "Who specifically . . . ?"
Rationale for Clarification Questions—By questioning, the teacher also gains insight into the person to whom the student is referring. Sensitivity to an individual's needs and personality is necessary in this type of questioning. Here, as with any clarification question, it is important to realize that in probing for accurate communication, you often uncover sensitive areas . Discretion and caution are advised.

UNSPECIFIED VERBS OR VAGUE VERBS

The unspecified or vague verb does not give a full descriptive meaning of the events. Verbs in this category are not explicit about the action as to how, when, or where. They force the listeners to supply the meanings from their own models of the world. This may result in miscommunication.

EXAMPLE 1
Student: "Jim ignores me."
Teacher: "**Specifically how** does Jim ignore you?"
Student: "He walks away and doesn't wait for me at the classroom door . "
Suggested Clarifications—"**Specifically how (when)** . . . ?"
Rationale for Clarifications—By questioning the student, the teacher gains a more detailed description of the verb. It also supplies a form of clarification for the student. It is interesting how information of this type can serve to limit "fortune telling" and other communication problems.

EXAMPLE 2
Student: "Martha keeps bothering me."
Teacher: "**How** does Martha bother you?"
Student: "She borrows my paper and doesn't return it."
Suggested Clarifications—"**How** does . . . ?" "**What** does . . . ?" "**When** does . . . ?"
Rationale for Clarifications—The teacher, by questioning the student, has clarified the meaning of the word "bother." If this had not been done, the teacher may have used his/her own personal frame of reference for the interpretation of the word "bother." "Bother" could have been interpreted as physical contact or verbal interaction. When communication channels are clear, many inappropriate reactions are eliminated, or at least put in proper perspective.

MODAL OPERATORS OR MUST WORDS

Modal operators or must words imply a required condition. They identify the limitations of the speaker's model of the world. Must words include: have to, must, must not, can't, cannot, ought to, ought not, etc. Eliminating modal operators gives choices and provides alternative responses to the student.

EXAMPLE 1

Student: "I can't try out for the debate team."

Teacher: "**What prevents** you from trying out?"

Suggested Clarifications—"**What prevents** you ... ?" "**What will happen if** you ... ?"

Rationale for Clarifications—Many times a student says, "I can't," because of a belief system which views the task as being beyond the student's ability. All too often, it is not the ability, but the belief, that impedes behavior. By using the clarification questions suggested above, the teacher can discover the perceived limitations. With this information, the teacher is in a better position to evaluate the student's belief system and plan an appropriate intervention.

EXAMPLE 2

Student: "I can't challenge Maryann to a debate."

Teacher: "**What would happen if** you did?"

Suggested Clarifications—"**What would happen** if you did ... ?" "**What prevents** you ... ?"

Rationale for Clarifications—In responding to the student, the teacher's question, "What would happen if you did?" opens up new areas of awareness. By questioning modal operators, the teacher gives the student an opportunity for additional choices and the opportunity for additional choices and the opportunity to discover alternative behaviors.

"ALL THE TIME FOOLERS" OR OVERGENERALIZATIONS

In this category, the speaker is caught using words that include all members of a class, allegedly possessing certain qualities. The speaker has generalized from one or several experiences or events to another experience or event. This overgeneralization limits a person's responses and the ability to make discriminations. Words include: all, ever, every, always, never, no one, nobody, none, everybody, each time, etc.

EXAMPLE 1

Student: "Nobody ever plays with me."

Teacher: **"Nobody ever** plays with you?" (Or, "Can you remember a time someone did play with you?")

Suggested Clarifications—Reflect back the **key word** in an exaggerated fashion, emphasizing it by tonality or volume. Use the counter approach by asking the student to remember a time that is in contrast to their statement e.g., "Has there ever been a time when someone played with you?"

Rationale for Clarifications—As the teacher identifies discrepancies in the student's view of the world, new areas of awareness are possible; and a student learns that many of their perceptions of the world are not reality-based.

EXAMPLE 2

Student: "You never, ever pay any attention to me."

Teacher: "I **never, ever, ever** pay attention to you?"

Student: "Well, maybe this morning when I came into class."

Suggested Clarifications—Reflect back the **key word** in an exaggerated fashion, emphasizing it by tonality or volume. Examples: never, ever, always, all. The counter approach also may be used by asking, "Was there ever a time I paid attention to you?"

Rationale for Clarifications—The teacher's use of exaggeration in the above example causes the student to reexamine his original statement. If questioning does not produce a desirable response, the teacher should question further, e.g., ". . . Was there ever a time . . . ?" Caution should be exercised in using exaggerated speech, as the student may mistake it for sarcasm.

FORTUNE TELLING OR MIND READING

In this category, the language illusion is that one individual can tell what another individual is thinking or feeling. The individual believes he can predict what the speaker is thinking or feeling without checking it out with the speaker. This category can cause misunderstanding and may create anger in the person to whom it is directed. Our culture provides numerous examples of people portraying that they are able to read other people's minds. Perhaps nowhere is it found more often than within the family structure. Children often hear their parents making statements such as, "John, don't tell me you didn't do that," or "I can tell what you are thinking—you are thinking about how to get out of this."

When we have a relationship with someone, we pick up patterns of that person's behavior, both consciously and unconsciously. As a result, we are able to predict their thinking or feeling some of the time. The basic problem is that even if you are right about the person's thinking or feeling fifty percent of the time, you are also wrong fifty percent of the time!

EXAMPLE 1
Student: "I know you're not going to like my term paper."
Teacher: "**How do you know** I'm not going to like your term paper?"
Suggested Clarifications: "**How do you know** . . . ?"
Rationale for Clarifications: In addition to stopping the fortune telling response with the student, the teacher can learn much from this type of clarification question. The teacher can gain important information on how that person views the world. By learning the frame of reference in which the student operates, the teacher will gain an understanding of the student and what the student's perceptions are about term papers and the teacher.

EXAMPLE 2
Student: "John doesn't like me."
Teacher: "**How do you know** John doesn't like you?"
Student: "It's simple. He never talks to me."
Suggested Clarification—"**How do you know** . . . ?"
Rationale for Clarification—In the above example, it is apparent that the clarification question has evoked the student's personal definition or criteria of "liking." By future questioning and clarifying, the teacher can assist the student in developing realistic perceptions and social skills. In the above example, it is apparent that much value can be gained if John is aware of his assumptions and perceptions. This clarification technique becomes very valuable when teachers work with students and parents.

CAUSE AND EFFECT OR "THIS CAUSES THAT"

Cause and effect is the belief that some action or part of one person can cause another person to experience emotion or change in a person's inner state. The person who uses this category believes there are no options and gives up power and responsibility for his/her own emotions or inner states.

EXAMPLE 1
Student: "You make me happy!"
Teacher: "**Specifically how** do I make you happy?"
Student: "You call on me and answer my questions."
Suggested Clarification—"**Specifically how** . . . ?"
Rationale for Clarification—By seeking out the specific behavior that the student has related to happiness, the teacher gains insight to the student's perception of happiness. In this example, happiness has been equated with attention. This may prove to be a valuable source of information for teachers in terms of identifying powerful reinforcers and punishers.

EXAMPLE 2
Student: "You frustrate me."
Teacher: "**How**, specifically, do I frustrate you?"
Suggested Clarification—"**How, specifically** . . . ?"
Rationale for Clarification—By asking for a causal relationship, the student is challenged to come up with specific information. The answer given not only improves and opens communication, but can be influential in modifying teacher behavior. Questions represented in the examples may lead the teacher to discover that these students do not know they are causing their own problems or frustration .

LOST PERFORMATIVES OR MORAL JUDGMENTS

Lost performatives or moral judgments place value judgments on behavior or things from the speaker's model of the world. The speaker uses his personal judgment and shifts it to the total members of a class. Moral judgment words include: good, bad, crazy, right, wrong, best, worst, false, etc.

EXAMPLE 1
Student: "State College is the best!"
Teacher: "**According to whom?**"
Student: "Mr. Jones, our guidance counselor."
Suggested Clarifications—"**According to whom?**" "**Who says . .
. ?**" "**For whom . . . ?**" "**How do you know?**"
Rationale for Clarifications—In the above example, the teacher,
by using the suggested clarification question, has identified the
source of the student's judgment. With this information, the
teacher can work in extending the student's model of the world
and allow for the re-evaluation of beliefs and the consideration of
other viewpoints.

EXAMPLE 2
Student: "It's wrong to question the teacher's judgment."
Teacher: "**Who says** it's wrong?"
Suggested Clarifications—"**Who says . . . ?**" "**For whom . . . ?** "
"**According to whom . . . ?**" "**How do you know?**"
Rationale for Clarifications—Clarifying lost performatives en-
able students to examine their belief systems and the belief
systems of others. It also acts as a check on false beliefs.

In summary, the above procedures will facilitate effective
communication with staff and students when used appropriately. They also will decrease significantly the number of problems due to communication errors. The procedures will also
prevent individuals from manipulating you by their vagueness.

Chapter 11
Neuro Linguistic Programming And The Future

ADVANCED ORGANIZER

In this final chapter, you will be given the opportunity to appreciate the potential of what you have accomplished in the preceding ten chapters. You will discover that you now have the knowledge to effect rapid and positive changes in your world and the world of those whom you teach. It is hoped that education, child rearing practices, the field of mental health, and other fields will profit with these new skills and by the release of the unlimited inner resources that individuals all possess. It remains for you to unlock these resources and maximize your contribution to yourself and the world.

NEURO LINGUISTIC PROGRAMMING AND THE FUTURE

In a complex, ever-changing world, where knowledge doubles every seven years, we are rapidly approaching a time when we must provide new approaches that will allow us to learn quickly and efficiently. Tedious, lengthy drills and "no gain without pain" are questionable and are methods of learning that are technologically out of date.

The potential of the human brain has not begun to be realized. Just a few years ago, it was thought that the four minute mile was untouchable. Today, it is commonplace. Our changing belief systems are opening up new possibilities. Educators at all levels across the country have begun to realize that there is a better way to educate people.

The courage to change and to try something different has opened up new worlds of possibilities. "Fire walking," which was thought to be for the few "sacred elite," is now taught in a short time to many "everyday" people. (See *Life* magazine, March, 1985.)

Mega training and NLP provide powerful tools for enhancing the learning powers of an individual. As you implement the knowledge and skills we have provided for you, you will find or discover many variations and adaptations for productive use. We invite you to share your examples and discoveries with us, so that we may extend them to others.

As you have read through these pages and experienced the powerful technology contained therein, you have probably reflected on your own personal history. In so doing, you have undoubtedly identified situations when you have unconsciously or consciously utilized the principles of Neuro Linguistic Programming. There were probably other situations where, in retrospect, you could see the value of the techniques had they been known.

The serious question is, "What is to come in the future?" Many of us have a "mind set" which we use in looking forward to future situations. All too often, this mind set is a reflection on the past, which brings with it a concentration on what has not worked rather than what has been successful.

In this regard, it might be well to shake out our old belief systems and make space for what can, and most probably will, be possible within the next twenty years. While we realize that long range predictions can prove to be most embarrassing, we also realize that, without dreams and realistic projections, a society can sink into stagnation by the perpetuation of long-held fallacious beliefs. How many of our beliefs might be the product, not of reality, but of the limitations of our belief systems? We must allow ourselves to envision what may be possible and not limit ourselves to what we see today.

The fresh look at the potential in education suggested by this text is a case in point. Why should the acquisition of a body of knowledge contained in our schooling experience be so painful or time-consuming? If one were to synthesize the basic minimum of an eight year grammar school education and a four year high school experience, it would be apparent that a great deal of time is really wasted. The content material, if consolidated, might well be learned by a "motivated" student in less than one-third the time. Many readers of this statement may be shocked by this position, feeling (quite justifiably) that there is more to education than just content. With this observation, the authors would readily agree.

It is conceivable that, during their education, many students are learning all sorts of responses. They are learning to fear learning, to escape responsibility, to depreciate their own true values, etc. It is impossible for any individual to go through an experience that involves eight hours a day, forty weeks a year, for twelve years without displaying a marked change in behavior. Just because the schools do not plan undesirable learning responses does not mean they do not occur.

As we have learned, anchors or associations can occur at any time and the true meaning of communication is the response it brings forth. Since this is reality and cannot be changed by rhetoric, let us look to the future and view the educational world through NLP.

Given the fact that individual differences, rapport and communications are considered by all to be the most important aspects of education, it is of primary importance to address this area first. While all agree to the importance of these variables, very few (if any) researchers specify what they are or how they are to be realized. Individual differences are more than standard deviations and test scores.

When educators realize that each one of us has our own "model of the world," and this model is the reality as each of us perceives it, what a difference in education there will be! To be sure, there will not only be research into how an individual acquires these specific models, but more importantly, attention will be paid to meeting individuals at their models of the world. Increased rapport and subsequent effective communication would be the natural outcomes. Society would gain from the individual nature of each person's viewpoint.

Schooling itself would change. Once research has determined the most effective learning strategies for each area, the student would be guided to adopt the most effective means of acquiring basic information. More important would be the development of improved accessing techniques. While information is important, the means of retrieval is of primary concern. With the volume of knowledge doubling every seven years, not only is acquisition important, but retrieval becomes vital. NLP's recognition and attention to these important variables have the potential of revitalizing education at all levels.

Appendices

APPENDIX 1

SORTING GUIDE QUESTIONNAIRE

This Sorting Guide Questionnaire can be used to identify student interests and reinforcers. Interests are identified for the purpose of communicating to students in terms of their individual interests. This will build rapport and a relationship. Interests also can be woven into subject matter to increase motivation. Reinforcers can be gleaned from interests and used to reinforce desirable student behavior and learning.

DIRECTIONS: The teacher should inform the students that this questionnaire is designed to help the teacher know and understand the student better. It is also designed to find out what the student's interests are and what is reinforcing to the student. The teacher should tell the student that there are no right or wrong answers to the questions. The answers are unique to each student. The teacher should write the answers given by the student under the questions or on a separate sheet of paper. The teacher should feel free to further question the student about the answers given to the questions. The idea is to evoke information concerning interest patterns and reinforcement preferences of that student. The teacher should read verbatim the following questions to students:

1.   Name three things that make you happy.
2.   Name three things you like to do in your spare or free time.
3.   Name three things you like to buy.
4.   What games do you like?
5.   Who do you like to be with? Why?
6.   Do you have any hobbies?
7.   Do you belong to any clubs or organizations?
8.   Do you watch television? What programs?
9.   Do you go to the movies? What type of movies do you like best?
10. Do you listen to the radio? What type of music do you like best?
11. Do you read books, magazines, or the newspapers?
  a.   What type of books or stories do you like?
  b.   Do you have any books of your own?
  c.   What type of magazines do you like to read?
  d.   What sections of the newspapers do you like best?
12. Do you like to have someone read to you? If so, what would you like read to you?
13. What did you like to do when you were very young? (Would you like to do this now?)
14. Do you have any pets? Would you like a pet? What kind?
15. What have been interested in lately?
16. What school subjects do you like the best? Why?
17. What school subjects do you like the least? Why?

At this point, the teacher should look over the responses for patterns of interests and potential reinforcers. The teacher then should answer the following questions (record answers on a separate sheet of paper):

A. Does the Questionnaire show a pattern of interests? If so, group them.
B. Are there any interests that appear to be sustaining?
C. Looking at the interests, note how they could be used as reinforcers.
D. List the reinforcers gleaned from the interests. Consider them

as suspect reinforcers until they prove effective upon application to a given situation. If the desired behavior increases as a result of the applied suspect reinforcer, it is in actuality a reinforcer for that particular student. If the suspect reinforcer does not increase the behavior to which it is applied, it is to be dropped from the list. Using the same procedure, other reinforcers can also be tested for effectiveness.

APPENDIX 2

PREDICATES

VISUAL (SEE)	AUDITORY (HEAR)	KINESTHETIC (FEEL)
See	Hear	Feel
Looks	Sounds	Grip
Clear	Loud	Grasp
Focus	Listen	Warm
Perspective	Mention	Firm
Watch	Say	Emotional
Show	Earful	Solid
Foresee	Talk	Touch
Appear	Discuss	Sense
Picture	Remark	Move
View	Inquire	Turn
Sight	Vocal	Thrill
Recognize	Contact	Floating
Notice	Attentive	Irritate
Glance	Clam up	Sooth

APPENDIX 3

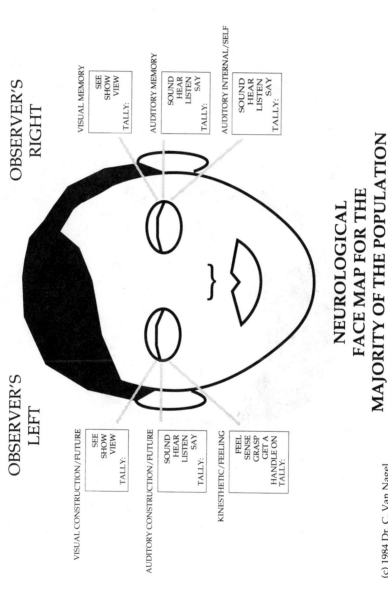

OBSERVER'S RIGHT

OBSERVER'S LEFT

VISUAL MEMORY
SEE
SHOW
VIEW
TALLY:

AUDITORY MEMORY
SOUND
HEAR
LISTEN
SAY
TALLY:

AUDITORY INTERNAL/SELF
SOUND
HEAR
LISTEN
SAY
TALLY:

VISUAL CONSTRUCTION/FUTURE
SEE
SHOW
VIEW
TALLY:

AUDITORY CONSTRUCTION/FUTURE
SOUND
HEAR
LISTEN
SAY
TALLY:

KINESTHETIC/FEELING
FEEL
SENSE
GRASP
GET A
HANDLE ON
TALLY:

NEUROLOGICAL
FACE MAP FOR THE
MAJORITY OF THE POPULATION

(c) 1984 Dr. C. Van Nagel

APPENDIX 4

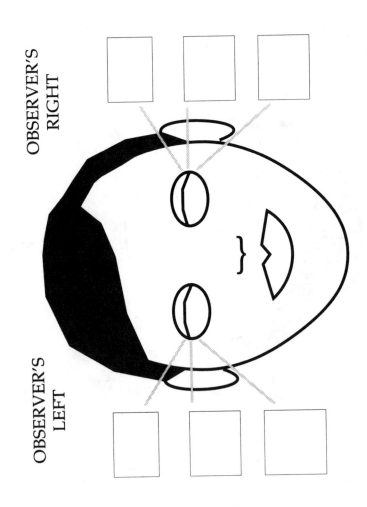

APPENDIX 5

QUESTIONS TO ELICIT
SPECIFIC EYE MOVEMENTS

VISUAL REMEMBERED IMAGES

1. What color are your mother's eyes?
2. What color is your (family) car?
3. Where did you see me first?
4. How many doors are in your home?
5. What color are the walls in your bedroom?
6. Who was the first person you saw today?
7. When was the last time you saw your own signature?
8. How many traffic lights did you pass on your way to school?
9. What color is your favorite shirt?
10. What color are the stars on our flag?

VISUAL CONSTRUCTED IMAGES

1. Imagine a purple cow.
2. Imagine yourself ten pounds lighter.
3. How much is 330 divided by 3?
4. Describe how you would look on a TV screen.
5. See a 757 airplane with props on the wings.
6. Imagine running for a touchdown in the Super Bowl.
7. Imagine a boat flying.
8. Imagine a dog with a beard.
9. What would a car with three wheels look like?
10. Imagine yourself with pink hair.

AUDITORY

1. Think of your favorite song—hum it to yourself.
2. Remember the conversation with the last person you were with last night.

3. How does your car engine sound?
4. Think of the sound of clapping at the last show you attended and hear it.
5. Distinguish between the sounds of a doorbell and a telephone bell.
6. Hear chalk as it is being used on the chalkboard.
7. Sing the song *Happy Birthday* inside your head.
8. Hear your mother calling you.
9. Hear an alarm clock go off.
10. Hear the sound of waves.

KINESTHETIC

1. Which is colder, your right arm or your left arm?
2. Feel the coldest snowball in your hands.
3. Feel the heat of hot sand on your feet.
4. Remember how you fe lt when you had your first kiss.
5. Remember the last time you felt really confident.
6. What does it feel like when you bite your tongue?
7. Feel your front teeth bite into an ice cream cone.
8. Feel yourself putting on a wet bathing suit.
9. What does it feel like to take a cold shower?
10. Feel the fur on a cat.

APPENDIX 6

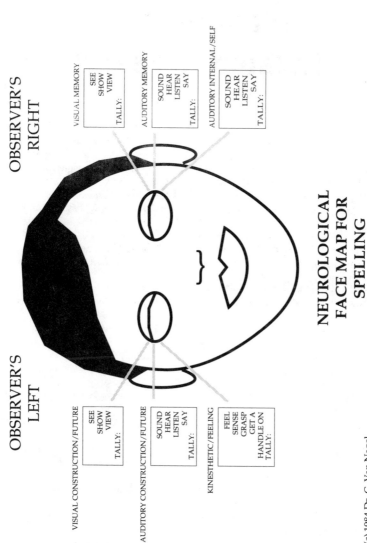

OBSERVER'S RIGHT

OBSERVER'S LEFT

VISUAL MEMORY

SEE
SHOW
VIEW
TALLY:

AUDITORY MEMORY

SOUND
HEAR
LISTEN
SAY
TALLY:

AUDITORY INTERNAL/SELF

SOUND
HEAR
LISTEN
SAY
TALLY:

VISUAL CONSTRUCTION/FUTURE

SEE
SHOW
VIEW
TALLY:

AUDITORY CONSTRUCTION/FUTURE

SOUND
HEAR
LISTEN
SAY
TALLY:

KINESTHETIC/FEELING

FEEL
SENSE
GRASP
GET A
HANDLE ON
TALLY:

NEUROLOGICAL FACE MAP FOR SPELLING

(c) 1984 Dr. C. Van Nagel

Bibliography/ Related Research

Andreas, C. "The Relationship of Eye Movements While Information Processing to Sensory Mode." University of Colorado: Unpublished doctoral dissertation, 1983.

Appel, P. R. "Matching of Representational Systems and Interpersonal Attraction." United States International University: Dissertation, 1983.

Asbell, H. C. "Effects of Reflection, Probe, and Predicate-Matching on Perceived Counselor Characteristics." University of Missouri at Kansas City: Dissertation, 1983.

Aspy, D. N. & Roebuck, F. N. *Kids Don't Learn from People They Don't Like.* Amherst, MA: Human Resources Development Press, 1977.

Baer, D. M., Peterson, R. F., & Sherman, J. A. "The Development of Imitation By Reinforcing Behavioral Similarity To A Model," *Journal of the Experimental Analysis of Behavior,* 10 (1967), 405-416.

Bandler, R & Grinder, J. *Frogs Into Princes.* Moab, UT: Real People Press, 1979.

Bandler, R., Grinder, J. & Satir, V. *Changing With Families.* Palo Alto, CA: Science and Behavior Books, Inc., 1976.

Bandura, A. *Principles of Behavior Modification.* NY: Holt, Rinehart and Winston, 1969.

Barbe, W. B., Swassing, R. H., & Milone, M. N. *Teaching Through Modality Strengths: Concepts and Practices.* Columbus, OH: Zaner-Bloser, 1979.

Blakeslee, T. R. *The Right Brain: A New Understanding of the Unconscious Mind and Its Creative Process.* NY: Berkley Books, 1983.

Bontrager, C. "General Semantics." California, PA: Lecture given at California State College, 1961.

Boswell, L. K. Jr. "The Initial Sensitizing Event Of Emotional Disorders," *British Journal of Medical Hypnotism,* 12 (3) (1961).

Bower, G. H. "Mood and Memory," *American Psychologist,* 36 (2) (1981), 129-148.

Bracht, G. H. "Experimental Factors Related To Aptitude-Treatment Interactions," *Review of Educational Research,* 40 (1970), 627-641.

Brockman, W. P. "Empathy Revisited: The Effect Of Representational System Matching On Certain Counseling Process And Outcome Variables." (The College of William and Mary in Virginia.) In Dissertation Abstracts International (1981) 41 (8), 3421A.

Buckner, Michael, et al. "The Use of Eye Movement as an Indicator of Visual Components in Thought," *Journal of Counseling Psychology,* Vol. 34, No. 3 (1987), 283-287.

Burnes, F. & Nelson, L. "High Performance Programming: An Operations Model For A New Age," O E Communique: The Professional Organization, Effectiveness, Development Publications of the U. S. Army, 512, 27 (1981).

Burton, J. K. & Brunning, R. H. "Interference Effects On The Recall Of Pictures, Printed Words, And Spoken Words," *Contemporary Educational Psychology*, 7 (1982), 61-69.

Buzan, T. *Use Both Sides of Your Brain*. New York: E. P. Dutton, 1976.

Campos, L. "Using Metaphor For Identifying Life Script Changes," *Transactional Analysis Journal*, 2 (2) (1972), 75.

Carrier, C., Karbo, K., Kindem, H., Legisa, G., & Newstrom. Use Of Self-Generated And Supplied Visuals As Mnemonics In Gifted Children's Learning," *Perceptual and Motor Skills*, 57 (1) (1983), 235-240.

Chalfant, J. C. & Scheffelin, M. A. *Central Processing Dysfunctions in Children: A Review of Research*. U. S. Dept. of Health, Education, and Welfare, National Institute of Neurological Diseases and Stroke, 1969.

Cody, S. G. "Stability and Impact of the Primary Representational System in Neurolinguistic Programming: A Critical Examination." University of Connecticut: Dissertation, 1983.

Cooper, J. C. & Gaeth, J. H. "Interactions Of Modality With Age And With Meaningfulness in Verbal Learning," *Journal of Educational Psychology*, 58 (1976), 41-44.

Denholtz, M. S. & Mann, E. T. "An Automated Audiovisual Yreatment Of Phobias Administered By Non-Professionals," *Journal of Behavior Therapy and Experimental Psychiatry*, 6 (1975), 111-115.

Dilts, R. *Applications of Neuro Linguistic Programming*. Cupertino, CA: Meta Publications, 1982.

Dilts, R. *Roots of Neuro Linguistic Programming*. Cupertino, CA: Meta Publications, 1982.

Dilts, R. B. *Neuro-Linguistic Programming in Education: Building Blocks for Learning*. Scotts Valley, CA: Behavioral Engineering, 1980.

Dilts, R., Bandler, R., Grinder, J., Bandler, L. C. & DeLozier, J. *Neuro Linguistic Programming, Vol. I*. Cupertino, CA: Meta Publications, 1980.

Dowd, E. T., & Petty, J. "Effect of Counselor Predicate Matching On Perceived Social Influence And Client Satisfaction," *The Journal of Counseling Psychology*, 30 (1982), 339-345.

Dunn, R., Dunn, K. & Price, G. *Learning Style Inventory*. Lawrence, KS: Price Systems, 1975.

Ellickson, J. L. "The Effect Of Interviewers Responding Differentially To Subjects' Representational Systems As Indicated By Eye Movement." (Michigan State University: Doctoral dissertation.) Dissertation Abstracts International, 41 (7) (1980), 2754B.

Ellis, A. *Reason and Emotion in Psychotherapy*. NY: Lyle Stuart, 1962.

Erickson, M., & Rossi, E. *Indirect Forms Of Suggestion. In The Collected Papers of Milton Erickson on Hypnosis*. NY: Irvington, 1980.

Eriksen, C. C., L Kuethe, J. L. "Avoidance Conditioning of Verbal Behavior Without Awareness: A paradigm of Repression," *Journal of Abnormal Social Psychology*, 55, (1956) 203-209.

Falzette, W. C. "Matched Versus Unmatched Primary Representational Systems And Their Relationship To Perceived Trustworthiness In A Counseling Analogue," *Journal of Counseling Psychology*, 28 (1981), 305-308.

Farmer, S. S. (1984). "Supervisory Conferences in Communicative Disorders: Verbal and Nonverbal Interpersonal Communication Pacing." (University of Colorado at Boulder: a dissertation.) Dissertation Abstracts International, 44 (9) (1984), 27815B.

Ferguson, M. "NLP: A Science For Increasing Beneficial Choices," *Brain Mind Bulletin*, 7 (11) (1982), 1-3.

Flanders, N. A. *Cooperative Research: Teacher Influence, Pupil Attitudes, and Achievement, Monograph No. 12*. Washington, D. C.: U. S. Dept. of Health, Education, and Welfare, U. S. Government Printing Office, 1965.

Foreyt, J. P., & Hagen, R. L. "Covert Sensitization: Conditioning or Suggestion?" *Journal of Abnormal Psychology*, 82 (1973), 17-23.

Framingham, Massachusetts Study. National Institute of Health, 1972.

Frieden, F. P. "Speaking The Client's Language: The Effects of Neuro-Linguistic Programming (Predicate Matching) On Verbal And Nonverbal Behaviors In Psychotherapy— A Single Case Design." (Virginia Commonwealth University: Doctoral dissertation.) Dissertation Abstracts International, 42 (3) (1981), 1171B.

Gaudry, E., & Spielberger, C. D. *Anxiety and Educational Achievement*. NY: Wiley, 1971.

Gelzheiser, L. M., Solar, R. A., Shepherd, M. J., Wozniak, R. H. "Teaching Learning Disabled Children To Memorize: A Rationale For Plans And Practice," *Journal of Learning Disabilities*, 16 (7) (1983), 421-425.

Goldfried, M. R., Decenteceo, E. T., & Weinberg, L. "Systematic Rational Restructuring As A Self-Control Technique," *Behavior Therapy*, 5 (1974), 247-254.

Goldfried, M. R., & Goldfried, A. P. *Cognitive Change Methods. In F. H. Kanfer and A. P. Goldfried (Eds.), Helping People Change*. NY: Pergamon, 1975.

Goldfried, M. R., Linehan, M. M., & Smith, J. L. "The Reduction of Test Anxiety Through Rational Restructuring," *Journal of Consulting and Clinical Psychology*, in press (1985).

Goleman, D. "People Who Read People," *Psychology Today* (July, 1979).

Gordon, D. *Therapeutic Metaphors: Helping Others Through the Looking Glass*. Cupertino, CA: Meta Publications, 1978.

Goulding, R. L., & Goulding, M. *The Power Is In The Patient*. San Francisco, CA: T. A. Press, 1978.

Goulding, R. L., & Goulding, M. "Injunctions, Decisions, And Redecisions," *Transactional Analysis Journal*, 6 (1) (1976), 41-48.

Gregorc, A. F. *Learning/Teaching Styles: Their Nature And Effects. In Student Learning Styles*, pp. 19-26. Reston, VA: National Association of Secondary School Principals, 1979.

Groninger, L. D., & Groninger, L. K. "Function of Images In The Encoding-Retrieval Process," *Journal of Experimental Psychology: Learning, Memory, and Cognition*, 8 (4) (1982), 353-358.

Hammer, A. L. "Matching Perceptual Predicates: Effect On Perceived Empathy In A Counseling Analogue," *Journal of Counseling Psychology*, 30 (1983), 172-179.

Hammer, A. L. "Language As A Therapeutic Tool: The Effects On The Relationship Of Listeners Responding To Speakers By Using Perceptual Predicates." Dissertation Abstracts International, 41 (3) (1980).

Hanna, R., Hodges, R., & Hanna, J. *Spelling Structure and Strategies*. Boston: Houghton-Mifflin, 1971.

Hanna, R., Hanna, J., Hodges, R., & Rudorf, E. *Phoneme-Grapheme Correspondence as Cues to Spelling Improvement*. Washington, D. C.: U. S. Dept. of Health, Education, and Welfare, OE 32008, 1966.

Haynie, N. A. "Systematic Human Relations Training with Neuro Linguistic Programming." University of Georgia: Dissertation, 1981.

Hefele, T. T. "The Effects Of Systematic Human Relations Training Upon Student Achievement," *Journal of Research and Development in Education*, 4 (1971), 52-69.

Hernandez, V. O. "A Study Of Eye Movement Patterns In The Neurolinguistic Programming Model." (Ball State University: Doctoral dissertation). Dissertation abstracts International, 42 (4) (1981), 1587B.

Higgins, H. L. "The Conditioned Reflex Of Pavlov: Practical Clinical Applications, Especially To Children," *New England Journal of Medicine*, 225 (1941), 772-775.

Hill, E. L. "An Empirical Test Of The NLP Concept Of Anchoring." Dissertation Abstracts International, 44 (7) (1984), 2246B.

Hortin, J. A., & Bailey, G. D. "Visualization: Theory And Applications For Teachers," Reading Improvement, 20 (1) (1983), 70-74.

Hupp, D. Neurolinguistic Programming and Unconscious Learning Pathways. Available from NLP Institute of D. C., 380 Maple Ave., West Vienna, VA 22190, 1981.

Jacobson, S. Meta-Cation. Cupertino, CA: Meta Publications, 1983.

Janis, I. L., & King, B. T. The Influence Of Role Playing On Opinion Change," Journal of Abnormal and Social Psychology, 49 (1954), 211-218.

Jones, J. P. Intersensory Transfer, Perceptual Shifting, Model Preference, and Reading. Newark, DE: International Reading Association, 1972.

Jones, R. Self-fulfilling Prophecies: Social, Psychological, and Physiological Effects of Expectancies. NY: Wiley, 1977.

Kimmel, H. D. "Instrumental Conditioning Of Automatically Mediated Responses In Human Beings," American Psychologist, 29 (1974), 325-335.

Kozybski, A. Science and Sanity. NY: International Non-Aristotelian Library, 1958.

Kunen, S., & Duncan, E. M. "Do Verbal Descriptions Facilitate Visual Inferences?" Journal of Educational Research, 76 (6) (1983), 370-373.

Kunen, S., Green, D., & Waterman, D. Spread Of Encoding Effects Within The Nonverbal Visual Domain," Journal of Experimental Psychology: Human Learning and Memory, 5 (6) (1979), 574-584.

Lacey, J. I., & Smith, R. L. "Conditioning And Generalization Of Unconscious Anxiety," Science, 120 (1954), 1045-1052.

Lankton, S. R. Practical Magic: The Clinical Applications of Neuro Linguistic Programming. Cupertino, CA: Meta Publications, 1979.

Leffel, G. M. The Role of Metaphor in Human Behavior. Point Loma College: Graduation with Distinction Project, 1977.

Lin, N. The Study of Human Communication. NY: The Bobbs-Merrill Co., Inc., 1973.

Lockhard, J., L Sidowski, J. B. "Learning In Fourth And Sixth Graders As A Function Of Sensory Modes Of Stimulus Presentation And Overt Or Covert Practice," Journal of Educational Psychology, 52 (1961), 262-265.

Mace, S. "The Eyes Have It: NLP Learning Theories Inspire Spelling Program," Info World, March 22, 8 (1982).

Mattar, A. T. "Primary Representational Systems As A Basis For Improved Comprehension And Communication." (Utah State University: Doctoral dissertation.) Dissertation Abstracts International, 41 (8) (1981), 3162B.

Mehrabian, A. Non-verbal Communication. NY: Aldine-Atherton, 1972.

Meichenbaum, D., & Cameron, R. Modifying What Clients Say To Themselves. In Mahoney, M. J., L Thoreses, C. E., Self-Control: Power to the Person. Monterey, CA: Brooks/Cole, 1974.

Mercier, M. A., & Johnson, M. "Representational System Predicate Use And Convergence In Counseling: Gloria Revisited," Journal of Counseling Psychology, 31 (1984), 161-169.

Miller, G. "The Magic Number Seven, Plus or Minus Two: Some Limits On Our Capacity For Processing Information," The Psychological Review, 63 (March, 1956).

Mills, R. E. Learning Methods Test. Ft. Lauderdale: The Mills School, 1970.

Mozingo, L. L. "An Investigation of Auditory and Visual Modality Preferences for Teaching Word Recognition Skills to Students Classified as Auditory or Visual Learners." University of South Carolina: Doctoral dissertation (1978).

Nagel, C. V. *How to Organize and Manage Your Classroom*. Jacksonville, FL: Super Learning Systems, 1985.

Nagel, C. V. *Van Nagel Diagnostic Series: Pinpointing a Student's Functioning in Reading, Writing, and Arithmetic*. Jacksonville, FL: Super Learning Systems, 1979.

O'Connor, R. "Modification of Social Withdrawal Through Symbolic Modeling," *Journal of Applied Behavior Analysis*, 2 (1969), 15-22.

O'Neal, H. Jr. *Learning Strategies*. NY: Academic Press, 1978.

Ong, J., L Jones, L. "Memory For Designs, Intelligence, And Achievement of Educable Mentally Retarded Children," *Perceptual and Motor Skills*, 55 (2) (1982), 379-382.

Ott, J. N. *Health and Light: The Effects of Natural and Artificial Light on Man and Other Living Things*. Old Greenwich, CT: The Derair-Adair Company, 1973.

Otto, W., McMenemy, R., & Smith, R. *Corrective and Remedial Teaching (2nd ed.)*. Boston: Houghton-Mifflin (1973), 254-255.

Palubeckas, A. J. "Rapport In The Therapeutic Relationship And Its Relationship To Pacing." Dissertation Abstracts International, 42 (6) (1981), 2543-4B.

Pantin, H. M. "The Relationship Between Subjects' Predominant Sensory Predicate Use, Their Preferred Representational System And Self-Reported Attitudes Towards Similar Versus Different Therapist-Patient Dyads." (University of Miami: Doctoral dissertation). Dissertation Abstracts International, 43 (7) (1983), 2350B.

Patterson, G. R. *An Application of Conditioning Techniques To The Control of A Hyperactive Child. In Ullmann, L. P., & Krasper (eds.), Case Studies in Behavior Modification, 370-375.* NY: Holt, Rinehart and Winston, 1965.

Patterson, G. R., McNeal, S., Hawkins, N., & Phelps, R. "Reprogramming The Social Environment," *Journal of Child Psychology and Psychiatry*, 8 (1967), 181-195.

Perelle, I. V. "Auditory And Written Visual Stimuli As Factors In Learning And Retention," *Reading Improvement*, 1 (1975), 15-22.

Rachman, S. "Clinical Applications of Observational Learning, Imitation, And Modeling," *Behavior Therapy*, 3 (1972), 379-397.

Reese, Maryann & Yancer, Carol. *Practitioner Manual For Introductory Patterns of NLP*. Indian Rocks Beach, FL: Southern Institute Press, Inc., 1986.

Reese, Maryann. *Walk What You Talk: Your Personal NLP Development Manual*. Indian Rocks Beach, FL: Southern Institute Press, Inc., 1989.

Restak, R. *The Brain*. NY: Bantam Books, 1984.

Richard, H. C., Dignam, P. J., & Horner, R. F. "Verbal Manipulation In A Psychotherapeutic Relationship," *Journal of Clinical Psychology*, 16 (1960), 364-367.

Rimm, D. C., & Litrak, S. B. "Self Verbalization And Emotional Arousal," *Journal of Abnormal Psychology*, 74 (1969), 181-187.

Rudolf, G. de M. "Deconditioning And Time-Therapy," *Journal of Mental Science*, 107 (1961), 1097-1101.

Salter, A. *A Conditioned Reflex Therapy: The Direct Approach to the Reconstruction of Personality*. NY: Putman (1961).

Sandhu, D. D. "The Effects of Mirroring Vs. Non-Mirroring of Clients' Trustworthiness, And Positive Interaction In Cross-Culture Counseling Dyads." Dissertation Abstracts International, 45 (4) (1984), 1042A.

Schmedlen, G. W. "The Impact of Sensory Modality Matching of Rapport In Psycho-Therapy." (Kent State University: Doctoral dissertation.) Dissertation Abstracts International, 42 (5) (1981), 2080B.

Seham, M. "The 'Conditioned Reflex' In Relation To Functional Disorders In Children," *American Journal of Disabled Children*, 43 (1932), 163-186.

Shobin, M. A. "An Investigation of The Effect of Verbal Pacing On Initial Therapeutic Rapport." (University of Boston: dissertation.) Dissertation Abstracts International, 41 (5) (1980), 1960A.

Singer, R. D. "Verbal Conditioning And Generalization of Pro-Democratic Responses," *Journal of Abnormal Social Psychology*, 63 (1961), 43-46.

Skinner, B. F. *Science and Human Behavior*. NY: Macmillan, 1953.

Staats, A. W., & Staats, C. K. "Attitudes Established By Classical Conditioning," *Journal of Abnormal Social Psychology*, 57 (1958), 37-40.

Stewart, J., & D'Angelo, G. *Together: Communicating Inter-personally*. London: Addison-Wesley, 1975.

Strayhorn, J. M. *Talking It Out*. Champaign: Research Press Co., 1977.

Suedfeld, P. "Attitude Manipulation In Restricted Environments: V. Theory and Research." Symposium paper read at XXth International Congress of Psychology, Tokyo, 1972.

Taffel, C. "Anxiety And The Conditioning of Verbal Behavior," *Journal of Abnormal Social Psychology*, 51 (1955), 496-501.

Tessler, R. C., & Schwartz, S. H. "Help Seeking Self-esteem, And Achievement Motivation: An Attributional Analysis," *Journal of Personality and Social Psychology*, 21 (1972), 318-326.

Tetlock, P. E., & Suedfeld, P. "Inducing Belief Instability Without A Persuasive Message: The Roles of Attitude Centrality, Individual Cognitive Differences, And Sensory Deprivation," *Canadian Journal of Behavioral Sciences*, 8 (1976), 324-333.

Ullmann, L. P., Krasner, I., & Collins, B. J. "Modification of Behavior Through Verbal Conditioning: Effects In Group Therapy," *Journal of Abnormal Social Psychology*, 62 (1961), 128-132.

Vander, Z. "The Effects of Meta-Model Questioning And Empathic Responding On Concreteness In Client Statements And Client Trustworthiness." Dissertation Abstracts International, 44 (12) (1984), 3600-3601A.

Van Mondfrans, A. P., & Travers, R. M. "Learning of Redundant Material Through Two Sensory Modalities," *Perceptual and Motor Skills*, 19 (1964), 743-751.

Warren, C. A. B. "The Use of Stigmatizing Labels In Conventionalizing Deviant Behavior.," *Sociology and Social Research*, 58 (1974), 303-311.

Webster, M. New Collegiate Dictionary. Springfield MA: G & C Merriam Co., 1984.

Willer, B., & Miller, G. H. "Client Involvement In Goal Setting And Its Relationship To Therapeutic Outcome," *Journal of Clinical Psychology*, 32 (1976), 689-690.

Wolpe, J. *The Practice of Behavior Therapy*. NY: Pergamon, 1969.

Wolpe, J. *Psychotherapy By Reciprocal Inhibition*. Stanford, CA: Stanford University Press, 1958.

Index

Metamorphous Press

Metamorphous Press is a publisher of books and other media providing resources for personal growth and positive change. MP publishes leading-edge ideas that help people strengthen their unique talents and discover that we are responsible for our own realities.

Many of our titles center around Neurolinguistic Programming (NLP). NLP is an exciting, practical, and powerful communication model that has been able to connect observable patterns of behavior and communication and the processes that underlie them.

Metamorphous Press provides selections in many useful subject areas such as communication, health and fitness, education, business and sales, therapy, selections for young persons, and other subjects of general and specific interest. Our products are available in fine bookstores around the world.

Our distributors for North America are:

Baker & Taylor	M.A.P.S.	Pacific Pipeline
Bookpeople	Moving Books	the distributors
Ingram	New Leaf	Sage Book Distributors
Inland Book Co.		

For those of you overseas, we are distributed by:

Airlift (UK, Western Europe)
Specialist Publications (Australia)

New selections are added regularly and availability and prices change, so call for a current catalog or to be put on our mailing list. If you have difficulty finding our products in your favorite bookstore, or if you prefer to order by mail, we will be happy to make our books and other products available to you directly. Please call or write us at:

Metamorphous Press
P.O. Box 10616 Portland, OR 97210-0616
TEL (503) 228-4972
FAX (503) 223-9117

TOLL FREE ORDERING
1-800-937-7771

MetamorpHous
AdvancEd
ProducT
ServicEs

MetamorpHous AdvancEd ProducT ServicEs (M.A.P.S.) is the master distributor for Metamorphous Press and other fine publishers.

M.A.P.S. offers books, cassettes, videos, software, and miscellaneous products in the following subjects; Bodywork, Business & Sales; Children; Education; Enneagram; Health; (including Alexander Technique and Rolfing); Hypnosis; Personal Development; Psychology (including Neurolinguistic Programming); and Relationships/Sexuality.

If you cannot find our books at your favorite bookstore, you can order directly from M.A.P.S.

TO ORDER OR REQUEST A FREE CATALOG

MAIL   M.A.P.S.
          P.O. Box 10616
          Portland, OR 97210-0616

FAX   (503) 223-9117

CALL   Toll free 1-800-233-MAPS

CUSTOMER SERVICE AND ALL OTHER BUSINESS

CALL   (503) 228-4972